What people are sayin

Rounding the Wheel of the Year

In *Rounding the Wheel of the Year* Lucya Starza brings into focus the idea that magic pervades the entire year, every day, and not just aggregate into eight isolated clusters, eight bulges spread on the circumference of a wheel. Through the research material, stories, and materials offered for practical purposes, the author conveys not only the message, but the feeling that celebrations follow along seasonal changes rather than with the dates set in the calendar. *Rounding the Wheel of the Year* is filled with delightful meditations, arts and crafts ideas, and activities to keep the joy alight every single day– whatever the time of year.
Daniela Simina, author of *Where Fairies Meet: Parallels Between Irish and Romanian Fairy Traditions* and *A Fairy Path: The Memoir of a Young Fairy Seer in Training*

Lucya Starza's *Rounding the Wheel of the Year* is a thoughtful exposition on one of the common structures in paganism: the Wheel of the Year. While acknowledging that the individual might celebrate in different ways, this book offers clear ways to celebrate the movement of light and dark. I appreciated the detailed offerings to support the energy of each calendar month and know a reader will too!
Irisanya Moon, author of *Gaia – Saving Her, Saving Ourselves*

Rounding the Wheel of the Year by Lucya Starza will help any reader engage with the spirit of each season. As well as suggesting ways to honour the festivals of the eight-fold wheel, Starza casts a wider net and suggests ways the reader can honour the passing of each season. More modern observances, such as Earth Day, are considered alongside festivals with ancient roots. Whether you want to undertake a guided visualisation or get out into nature and brush up on your plant and flower lore, this book is the perfect guide for changing times.

Andrew Anderson, author of *The Ritual of Writing, Artio and Artaois* and *The Magic of Cats*.

Pagan Portals

Rounding the Wheel of the Year

Celebrating the Seasons in Ritual, Magic,
Folklore and Nature

Pagan Portals

Rounding the Wheel of the Year

Celebrating the Seasons in Ritual, Magic,
Folklore and Nature

Lucya Starza

**MOON
BOOKS**

Winchester, UK
Washington, USA

JOHN HUNT PUBLISHING

First published by Moon Books, 2023
Moon Books is an imprint of John Hunt Publishing Ltd., No. 3 East Street, Alresford
Hampshire SO24 9EE, UK
office@jhpbooks.net
www.johnhuntpublishing.com
www.moon-books.net

For distributor details and how to order please visit the 'Ordering' section on our website.

Text copyright: Lucya Starza 2022

ISBN: 978 1 78535 933 0
978 1 78535 934 7 (ebook)
Library of Congress Control Number: 2022945811

A CIP catalogue record for this book is available from the British Library.

Design: Lapiz Digital Services

UK: Printed and bound by CPI Group (UK) Ltd, Croydon, CR0 4YY
Printed in North America by CPI GPS partners

We operate a distinctive and ethical publishing philosophy in
all areas of our business, from our global network of authors to
production and worldwide distribution.

Contents

Previous Books

Candle Magic
A witch's guide to spells and rituals
978-1-78535-043-6 (paperback)
978-1-78535-044-3 (e-book)

Poppets and Magical Dolls
Dolls for spellwork, witchcraft and seasonal celebrations
978-1-78535-721-3 (paperback)
978-1-78535-722-0 (e-book)

Guided Visualisations
Pathways into wisdom and witchcraft
978-1-78904-567-3 (paperback)
978-1-78904-568-0 (e-book)

Scrying
Divination using crystals, mirrors, water and fire
978-1-78904-715-8 (paperback)
978-1-78904-716-5 (e-book)

About the Author

Lucya Starza is an eclectic witch living in London, England. Her earlier titles in the Pagan Portals series include *Candle Magic, Guided Visualisations, Poppets and Magical Dolls,* and *Scrying.* Lucya also edited the community book *Every Day Magic – A Pagan Book of Days* and has her own blog at www.badwitch.co.uk.

Acknowledgements

I would like to thank the following people for their help in writing this book, from proofreading and suggestions to encouragement: Angela Timms, Caitriona Horan MA, CJ Hooper, Claire Pingel, Daniel Mack, Gemma Zoe Jones, Jane Mortimer, John Davies, Dr Winnard, Katie Player, Lora Mack, Seldiy Bate and Trefor Wickens. I couldn't have done this without you.

Note
Nothing in this book is medical advice. Plant and herb lore are mentioned purely for folkloric, seasonal and environmental information purposes.

Introduction

This started life in a series of posts for the Moon Books Blog[1], written with the intention of compiling and editing them into a book. Here it is: *Pagan Portals – Rounding the Wheel of the Year*. I gave it this title because I wanted to cover magic and lore for each month as well as pagan celebrations and folkloric customs. Many books focus on the eight Wheel of the Year festivals: Imbolc, Spring Equinox, Beltane, Summer Solstice, Lammas, Autumn Equinox, Samhain, and Winter Solstice. They often describe when those festivals take place, what flowers or fruits to put on an altar, what deities to honour, and rites, spells or crafts to accomplish during ceremonies. However, they can pay less attention to what's happening on other days, weeks and months of the year. It's useful to have a set date to meet other pagans for a ritual, but every single day has its own magical energy. The wheel of the year turns smoothly, it doesn't clunk over eight bumpy cogs or have eight knobbly handles like a ship's wheel. So, although this book mentions the sabbats of modern pagan witchcraft, it also goes into other ways to honour the seasons. I should mention I'm using Wheel of the Year with caps when writing specifically about the eight-festival calendar, but wheel of the year when I'm writing more generally.

How the months and seasons change vary depending on where you are. I'm usually in London, England, but spend much time on the Sussex coast. That's only a couple of hours' travel, but I notice flowers bloom and fruits are ripe about a week later due to cooler temperatures near the sea. In other parts of the northern hemisphere the seasons could be much later or earlier than they are for me. In the southern hemisphere the summer and winter are reversed. Folkloric customs vary from area to area let alone from country to country. I didn't have the word allowance to cover all of England, let alone the entire world, so I've done what I recommend others do. I've looked closely at what happens in my local area as the year goes round with a few glances further afield. I hope my insights and examples encourage you to do the same where you live.

I'm not entirely sticking to pagan stuff. In this book I look at wider folk customs and culture, because I don't think modern paganism benefits from isolating itself from the rest of society. But, before smoothing the knobs off the Wheel of the Year, I'll look at its origins.

Origins of the Wheel of the Year

The concept of the Wheel of the Year with its eight festivals was inspired by historic customs and the astronomical calendar but isn't itself an ancient system. Ross Nichols, founder of modern Druidry, and Gerald Gardner, founder of the modern pagan religion Wicca, share the honour of devising it in the form we know today, but they used ideas that began in the 19th century.

Mythologist and fairy tale collector Jacob Grimm is often cited as starting the idea in his 1835 book *Teutonic Mythology*. He mentions Yule as being an important midwinter festival in ancient times and waxes lyrical that "Easter-fires, Mayday-fires, Midsummer-Fires with their numerous ceremonies carry us back to heathen sacrifices." In 1890, Sir James Frazer published *The Golden Bough*, which stated Beltane and Samhain were the most important Gaelic festivals because they marked the start of summer and winter respectively. Margaret Murray's 1921 *The Witch-Cult in Western Europe* tried to identify festivals celebrated by what she believed were surviving groups of historic pagan witches. She wrote that important coven meetings took place on the quarter days of Candlemas on February 2, Roodmas or May Eve on April 30, Lammas on August 1, and All Hallows Eve on October 31. Although Grimm, Frazer and Murray are now considered problematic from an academic history perspective, they were widely believed to be accurate in their day and were hugely influential in the development of modern paganism. Their books are still a fabulous source for creative inspiration.

Gerald Gardner's first attempt at writing a cohesive magical system, Ye Bok of ye Art Magical, mentions "rites for the main sabbats for the quarter days which opened the seasons" according to Professor Ronald Hutton in *The Triumph of the Moon*. Hutton writes that Ye Bok is the first place in which recognisable witchcraft-style seasonal ceremonies were described, "for the four festivals identified by Murray as the main witches' sabbats". They include purification rites and speeches for the priestess personifying a goddess plus material borrowed from other sources including Aleister Crowley's Gnostic Mass. It's worth noting these rituals were intended to be enacted by groups of witches rather than as public annual customs or accounts of what witches did in the past. Gardner's later book, *Witchcraft Today*, includes a Yule rite consisting of casting a circle, purification, and invoking the goddess into the high priestess.

Cambridge academic and Druidry revivalist Ross Nichols was a firm friend of Gardner. Both were members of modern druid groups and enjoyed naturist retreats[2]. According to popular legend, it was at a nudist resort in the mid-20th century that the two men finalised the form of the Wheel of the Year we know today. The location possibly influenced the recommendation that Wiccan rites are performed skyclad, or naked. Honestly, you don't have to take your clothes off to celebrate the seasons unless you want to.

Something New, Something Old

The Wheel of the Year has a mathematical symmetry that appeals to many. It's easy to remember and has some history and tradition. However, a glance at books on annual customs, such as Steve Roud's *The English Year* or Hutton's *The Stations of the Sun*, show there are many more than eight customary annual events of note. Nowadays there are generally three ways modern pagans choose to ritually celebrate the yearly cycle:

1. Using Gardner and Nichol's eight-spoke Wheel of the Year calendar.
2. Reconstructing, reviving or attempting a continuation of historic religious feast days or magical traditions.
3. Being eclectic and doing what feels right for each individual in their own place and time.

I spent many happy years in an initiatory Gardnerian Wiccan coven doing the first. I've taken part in reconstructionist rituals and have every respect for those who follow such paths. I love to take part in folkloric seasonal customs, some of which may have old origins. However, over the past few years as a solitary witch I've become increasingly eclectic – and that's the place in my heart this book wells from.

Rounding the Wheel of the Year isn't intended to be a collection of Druidic, Wiccan or similar modern pagan Wheel of the Year rituals, although I outline the basics of a Wheel of the Year ceremony with simple instructions for a circle rite in chapter 1. If you're looking for more ritual scripts, among those published by Moon Books I would recommend *A Ceremony for Every Occasion: The Pagan Wheel of the Year and Rites of Passage* by Siusaidh Ceanadach and *Grimoire of a Kitchen Witch* by Rachel Patterson. Ultimately, how you choose to mark the cycles of nature is up to you and those you work magic with. The wheel of the year has always turned as smoothly as the world is round, and always will until the end of time. As Hutton writes in *Queens of the Wild*, seasonal activities have always happened in one form or another. "Their actual name changed every few centuries, but the basic pattern of the wheel of the year endured, and was truly prehistoric."

I hope you enjoy *Rounding the Wheel of the Year*. Chapter 1 offers practical ways of following the seasons with observation, art, writing, crafting, gardening, magic, and ritual. The following chapters move around the months with folklore, plant lore, spellcraft, divination, festivals, pagan observances, deities and more. At the end there's a look at moving into the next year.

Chapter 1

Rolling with the Wheel of the Year

You can start reading this book and working with the seasons at any time, beginning with whatever month you like. I'd recommend looking at the introduction and this chapter, but after that you can turn to whatever part of year it is for you. Each chapter after this covers a month, but I had to choose a point on the wheel of the year to embark on my own writing journey. January is the first month in the Gregorian calendar, which most countries accept as standard in a secular sense. Nevertheless, various cultures, spiritual paths and magical traditions mark their year's start at other times. In ancient Ireland, Samhain was both the end of summer and the end of the year. Winter began after it, and some following a Celtic path use that reckoning. In Wicca and many other modern pagan traditions, the Winter Solstice – sometimes called Yule – is at the top of Wheel of the Year depictions, as it marks the rebirth of the sun. When I was deciding where to start my book, that was my first choice. However, I then thought about my own practice. January 1 is what I personally feel is my New Year's Day, and a time for my own new beginnings, so that's where the next chapter commences.

Opinions vary on when the seasons start more than when the year begins. Although most pagans nowadays count four seasons of spring, summer, autumn (fall for Americans) and winter, some stick to two. Some people regard the seasons as starting on the equinoxes and solstices – that's the astronomical definition – or centring on them. Weather forecasters or meteorologists divide the year into three-month sets based on average temperatures, with England's spring starting on March 1, summer on June 1, autumn on September 1 and winter on

December 1[1]. The third way is to observe changes in plants and animals, such as falling leaves and birds migrating. Again, what you do is your choice.

The Wiccan rede is: "Do what you will but harm none." Rede means advice, and I don't personally take it too literally. After all, it's difficult to do no harm at all, even unintentionally. However, I do hold with the general lifestyle advice of doing what you want so long as it's legal and ethical. When deciding what to take from this book, do things you want and ignore bits that don't resonate with you spiritually or magically. The pagan path should be one of joy as far as possible, taking delight in the natural world and changing seasons, celebrating them and honouring deities who call to you along the way.

Ways to Observe the Changing Seasons

The best way to see what's happening in the natural world each month is to go outdoors or look out if you can't get out. Noticing things with our own senses is better than reading about them, even if the weather's bad. If all you do each month is spend time recognising what's bare and what's blooming, that's a valid observance of how the wheel of the year turns. If you live in the countryside or work in agriculture, you'll notice those things as a matter of course, but I'm an urban pagan and sometimes have to remind myself to look at the trees, plants, and wildlife in the city as well as the manmade bits.

The wise old witch who trained me would say:

The first thing you do before writing a ritual for the Wheel of the Year is look out of the window. What can you see growing there? What's happening in nature? Use that for inspiration. Don't mention ripening apples if the blossom isn't on the tree yet.

It's good advice if you're following a more rounded wheel of the year journey too. Here are some other things you can do each month:

Journalling and Scrapbooking

I can't recommend journaling enough as a way of recording magical and spiritual work. Write down spells, rituals or divinations you do. Make notes about nature, the weather, your thoughts and feelings, as well as customs that interest you or you take part in. There's something lovely about using a beautiful paper notebook, but there's nothing wrong with doing it electronically either. I started writing A Bad Witch's Blog[2] as a personal journal as well as to share with others. You can include pictures and photos or keep them separately.

Scrapbooks are also a lovely visual way of preserving memories. You can put photos and pictures in them along with things such as pressed flowers, greeting cards, labels from gifts or purchases. You can add words, but the overall effect is a montage of images. Each page captures the mood of an event, a special day or a period of time – perfect for working with the wheel of the year. You can keep a scrapbook alongside a journal. I like traditional paper scrapbooks, but use apps if you prefer to be digital.

Take Photographs

Even if you don't want to write a journal or use a scrapbook you can still take photos and create albums. Nowadays we're lucky because we can take unlimited pictures and share them on social media if we want. Photos are great for recording the changing seasons. Try taking a picture of a tree from the same position every month – or even every week – to observe its cycles in action. Several of the crafts and other activities I suggest are ephemeral. Flowers wilt or dry, you will change things on altars, and seasonal food will be eaten. A photo keeps a record.

Grow Plants

You don't need a garden, although obviously it helps. You can grow plants from seed in pots or window boxes. Think about what you'd like to grow. It could be vegetables for cooking, herbs for spellwork, flowers to beautify your space, or wildlife-friendly plants to attract bees, butterflies and other creatures. Where you start will depend on the time of year, from planting in spring and watching things peek from the soil, picking flowers or harvesting in summer, collecting seeds in autumn, or cutting back dead stalks to make room for the next cycle. Even at Yule you could get a tiny real fir tree in a pot, tend it all year and watch it grow until the next December and onwards.

Create Mandalas from Natural Objects
Using flowers, leaves, berries and so on in this creative way gives a reason to venture outdoors. Collect things where permitted, then take them indoors and arrange them on a sheet of paper. Mandalas made each month from natural objects can reflect our feelings and how they change as well as celebrating what's happening over the seasons. If you do this each month, then again in different years, you can observe an annual pattern of similarities. Meditate on your work. Photograph it before the greenery fades. Add the pictures to a scrapbook, journal or digital album.

I'm using the term mandala loosely to mean a spiritually significant picture or pattern to meditate on. The original sense of the word comes from Hinduism and Buddhism as a reflection of the universe and the connectedness of life; my use is more eclectic. You could call it art for contemplation.

Draw or Paint
Sketching from life encourages looking closely at what you're drawing. You become more aware of the shapes of petals or leaves, for example. Adding colour means observing more. It doesn't matter what skill or talent you have. This isn't a competition – it's a means of becoming more intimately familiar with the natural world or other aspects of your spiritual path.

Art doesn't have to be realistic. You could draw what you feel, or how you visualise the outcome of spells. You could depict spirits, deities or lines of energy perceived with psychic vision which the camera won't record. Use your imagination to create magical art inspired by all your senses.

Make Poetry

One prompt is to jot down all the words or phrases you can think of inspired by a month. It could include folklore, the weather, what's happening in nature or your thoughts and feelings. Compose a poem using as many or few of those words or phrases as you like. Poetry doesn't have to rhyme unless you want it to. Japan has a tradition of poetry that specifically references the seasons, particularly Haiku. These are short poems of three lines, totalling 17 syllables. There are five syllables on the first and last lines, with seven in the middle. Sometimes a structure can help inspiration.

Colour Symbolism

Look at what colour or colours are most present each month in the quality of the light, the flowers in bloom, even the clothes you feel most drawn to wearing. Light candles of those colours, use those colours in what you paint, craft or put on an altar.

Seasonal Altars

An altar can be as simple or as complex as you wish. You don't need a huge space. It can be a shelf, a fireplace top, a window ledge, a box or, of course, a table. Put things on it that resonate with the time of year, such as anything of an appropriate colour including cloths, candles, candle holders or crystals. Pick seasonal flowers. If you honour a specific deity, put their image or statue on your altar, but you could also add images of other deities that seem suitable as well as pictures of ancestors or animals.

Seasonal Crafting

This book offers crafting suggestions, but you can go further. Find out about crafts traditional for your area, research folkloric customs or things made in the pagan path you follow. You can adapt practical magic to honour the seasons such as making a poppet, or doll, for each month. It doesn't have to be complicated. Use a gingerbread-person cookie cutter as a pattern to cut out a back and front from felt in an appropriate colour. Stitch around the edges of your doll, stuffing as you go with dried seasonal herbs, flowers, grasses or leaves. You could dry and use flowers from a seasonal mandala or altar. Afterwards paint, draw or embroider features on the face. Finally add any other adornments such as clothes, trinkets or further embellishments. Seasonal poppets can be put on altars or used in spells when you want the energy the doll represents.

Food and Drink

Supermarkets stock food from all over the world and we can have things that aren't in season where we live. However, eating more local produce can mean we live more sustainably as well as feel in touch with the cycle of the year. I realise budgets might not allow sourcing everything from farmers' markets, and circumstances might mean we can't grow veg ourselves, but considering the options helps boost awareness of what's available. Just having a salad of dandelion leaves picked in the spring, or a glass of local apple juice in the autumn is a start. You can put seasonal food and drink on altars to enjoy after you've finished a ritual or as part of a celebration and leave a little outside as an offering.

Explore Annual Customs

Use this book as a starting point for further research into seasonal customs. Find out about annual events in your area, such as agricultural or trade fairs, non-pagan religious festivals, and modern yearly customs such as fetes, open days or parades. While these might not be specifically pagan, they mark days or weeks in the year for communities. Think about how these activities make you feel. Research their history, as many customs that seem ancient actually aren't. Some started as Victorian romantic ideas about what folklore ought to look like.

Guided Visualisations

Sometimes called pathworkings, these are journeys we make in our minds using a script created to help us experience a story as though we're part of it. They're intended to help us know ourselves better as well as to attune ourselves to the cycles of nature. The nice thing is we can do them even if we can't physically get outdoors. In this book I've included a guided visualisation for each season. You'll find them in January, April, July and November – the months that don't have a Wheel of the Year festival – but you can do them any time. Have a go at writing your own, using imagery and symbolism from your other work following the year.

Rituals

You don't have to do rituals as part of your practice, but I believe they can help with getting into a suitable state of mind for magical work or be part of regular spiritual observance. Rituals can be as simple as setting out a sacred place in which to work, doing a short meditation or lighting a candle and stating your intent. You can do this every day, every week, every month, at the Wheel of the Year festivals (sometimes called sabbats), or when you feel the new season has arrived or needs celebrating. Many mainstream modern pagan paths give most importance to Wheel of the Year rites, as I mentioned earlier. If you're part of a pagan tradition such as Wicca or Druidry then by all means follow those teachings, but here's an outlined suggestion for a simple circle ritual inspired by my own style of solitary witchcraft:

- Clean your space by sweeping with a broom.
- Set up a seasonal altar.
- Light a candle if allowed, otherwise use a battery candle.
- Cast a circle with a wand or your finger by pointing at the candle, then going around your space sunwise (deosil) visualising light encircling you and keeping you safe.
- Raise magical energy by drumming, clapping, singing, chanting, or moving while visualising energy rising from the ground and/or descending from the sky.
- Say words to honour the season and deities, spirits or ancestors you work with. This could be a poem, prayer, hymn or simply state: "In this circle I honour XXX."
- Do magical, spiritual or psychic work such as spells, crafts, writing, meditation, visualisation, divination, praying or asking for blessings, giving thanks, or making offerings such as incense or libations.
- Thank any spirits, ancestors or deities who attended your rite.
- Release your circle by going around your space anticlockwise (widdershins) and visualising the circle opening and unused energy returning to the ground or sky.
- Ground by pressing your feet and hands on a solid surface, then have something to eat and drink.

Some people like to create sacred space and cast a circle before journaling, scrapbooking or any form of spiritual crafting, but it isn't essential. Do what brings you joy as the wheel turns.

Chapter 2

Making January Magical

The first month of the year is cold and grey in England. It feels like the heart of winter, even though daylight hours are increasing. It can be hard to do anything except stay indoors in the warm, but hopefully I can offer ideas for making January more magical.

One way of combatting the January blues is to each day try to recognise something that makes you happy. It doesn't have to be anything big. It could be a favourite mug, a book, food, an item of clothing, or the glow from a candle on an altar. If you've started a journal, write about things that spark moments of happiness; or take photos then print them and paste them into a scrapbook. Visualise the joy as strongly as you can and ask your book to keep it safe. If you're feeling down, look back through your journal or scrapbook and visualise the happy moment again.

List Your Ambitions

A friend introduced me to a way of making a list for the year ahead that I've found works. Her idea is not to make a single resolution, but list many things to do over the year. Include fun things like visiting new places, crafting projects, and magical intentions as well as career or personal development aims. You could include suggestions from the previous chapter. I've found that with a long list I always succeed at quite a few. You don't have to write your list of ambitions on the first day of the month. Any time in January is good, particularly around the full moon, or when the sun enters Aquarius, which is great for new ideas. In the community book *Every Day Magic – A Pagan Book of Days*, Brendan Howlin points out January is more a time for thinking than acting:

In the northern hemisphere, people are just becoming aware of the small growing spark of light of the returning Sun. Think about what you would like to grow in your life this year. Is there a personal goal that you would like to accomplish? Do you want to spend more time with your family and/or friends or less time? Now is the time to think about it, not do it, because it is the wrong time for doing, that time is Imbolc (February 1), which is why New Year's resolutions often fail.

Don't feel guilty if you try something from your list early on but it doesn't work at the first attempt. You haven't failed – you have until the end of the year to keep on trying. Be gentle with yourself and give yourself a second chance and a third. Three's a magic number, after all.

Three-Knot Spell
Here's a traditional three-knot spell to add magical energy to resolutions or wishes, aiming to help you fix your intentions. You need a piece of cord, string, wool or similar – even ribbon from a Yule parcel. I'm a fan of reusing things. Tie three knots in the cord. With the first knot visualise your first steps towards whatever you're wishing for. With the second visualise achieving your goal. With the third visualise the forces of the universe helping your wish become reality. You can say these words:

By knot of one, my spell's begun
By knot of two, my wish comes true
By knot of three, so mote it be.

You don't only have to use that spell in January. You can do it any time of year. Keep your cord safe – perhaps use it as a bookmark in your journal or scrapbook. After your wish has come true, thank the universe and untie the knots. It's always good to give an offering after making a wish and when your wishes have been granted. In January, one suitable offering is to put food and water out for birds and other wildlife.

Janus, Vesta and Mari Lwyd

Janus is the Roman god of beginnings, gates, transitions, time, duality, doorways, passages, and endings. He has two faces; one looks back at the year gone, and one looks forward. It's Janus this month's named after. The Romans honoured him at the beginning of every religious ceremony, but at the start of the year they would bake cakes of spelt flour and salt as an offering to the deity. They exchanged gifts of dried fruit and honey and wished each other well for the months to come. You can honour Vesta, Roman goddess of the hearth, at the end of January rites. Give thanks for the warmth of fires – including modern central heating – within the home.

Mari Lwyd means Grey Mare in Welsh. In South Wales there's a new year custom in which a decorated horse's skull, known as a Mari, is paraded. People follow the Mari and win access to houses and pubs along the way by improvised sing-offs. Once inside, there's food, drink and the exchange of best wishes. Nowadays this custom has grown in popularity and I've even taken part in London, organised through the city's Welsh Centre[1].

Plant Lore in the Heart of Winter

January can bring ice and snow in England, although less often these days due to climate change. Deciduous trees are bare, but there are signs of life. On walks, as well as red berries and evergreens, I look for early cherry blossom, winter jasmine and the first buds of these two magical plants:

Camellias

These originally came from China, where they've been cultivated for thousands of years, after a Chinese emperor discovered an infusion of *camellia sinensis* leaves was his favourite drink. This became known as tea. The tea plant and ornamental camellias are closely related, but not the same. The beautiful flowers are magically associated with wealth and abundance. Having a shrub in your front garden is supposed to ensure prosperity. Dried petals can be used in wealth spells.

Witch-Hazel
Forked twigs or rods of this small tree that flowers in late winter are traditionally used by dowsers or water witches for finding underground springs. You can also use divining rods to search for lost things. Hold the ends of the rods or forked twig loosely in your hands then walk around the area you're searching. If you feel the rods move, jump, dip or pull in your hands it's an indication you might have found what you're looking for.

Winter Guided Visualisation: The Frozen Garden
I based this guided visualisation on things I've seen in my own garden in January, but do the visualisation indoors for comfort. Themes include nature, wintery weather, water, and ice. Before starting, make sure you're seated in a safe place where you won't be disturbed.

Close your eyes. Take three deep breaths in and out and relax. Visualise the following:

Visualise putting on winter clothes then walking through a door out of a warm and cosy home into a garden on a clear, bright, frosty morning. The sun is shining, but outside the air is cold and glints of frost sparkle on everything. Look around. Most of the trees and hedges stand bare, yet some are evergreen. You glimpse a few bright berries among the brown stalks. Some flowers bloom in wintertime. Few and far between perhaps, but maybe you can spot them. The flowerbeds are mostly bare, but green shoots of early spring bulbs are starting to push their way through frozen soil. A crisp white coating of frost covers any blades of grass while last year's fallen leaves are also frost-rimed. Explore the garden. What do you see? What do you smell? What do you hear? What do you feel?

You spot a pool of water frozen over. Perhaps it's a puddle of rainwater, maybe it's a bird bath, or a pond or lake. You are drawn to look at it. The surface is covered with ice. It isn't plain though. Geometrical patterns run through the crystalline frozen water. The sun glints on the ice, making the patterns stand out and shimmer. Look at them. Are they a cohesive whole, or made up of unique and individual parts? Does any aspect draw your attention? Spend some time studying this.

After a while you spot something below the frozen water. Peer through the layer of ice into the dark, still liquid below the crystalline surface. What do you see there? Is it a natural thing, or man-made? Is it something meant for you? Perhaps it's something you had lost and have now rediscovered. Is it something that should be there? Do you want to break the ice and free it, or leave it? Decide if you will do anything, and if so, what. Visualise doing that.

Now, look at the item again. Does it seem different? If it's something you've retrieved, will you keep it or leave it in the garden?

Having acted as you feel is right, look up from the frozen pool. Look around the garden again, then make your way back to the doorway. Return indoors to the warm and cosy home.

When you are ready, take a deep breath, shake your fingers and toes, and open your eyes to the real world.

Have something to eat and drink to fully ground – perhaps a wintertime warming favourite. You could create a version of this visualisation for each month but describe and picture how the garden changes as the seasons turn.

Chapter 3

February Brings Hope

One thing I love about February is watching the twilight time creeping later. The sunsets and the sky just afterwards can be beautiful with bare trees silhouetted against pink and purple. The sight fills me with hope for the spring to come. In traditional folklore it indicates good weather the next day too. Twilight is perfect for magic and divination because it's one of those liminal times of the day when change is in the air, and the month is when the natural world is changing from winter. February's a short month, but there's an extra day in leap years. Tap into that energy to wish for change in your life.

Imbolc, Brigid and Candlemas

The festival starting the month is Imbolc in the modern pagan Wheel of the Year, marking the first stirrings of spring. But it can still be bitterly cold. After a hilltop Imbolc rite a few years back I wrote in my diary: "Just got back from a druid ritual. Have hot water bottle to thaw the icicles that are my legs." I enjoy outdoor celebrations, but Imbolc is usually the coldest; much colder than Winter Solstice. But getting outside in the cold months is as important as being outdoors in the summer sun as it lets us experience all the seasons rather than just the pleasant ones.

Imbolc is almost certainly pre-Christian in origin according to Professor Ronald Hutton in *The Stations of the Sun*, although he points out that literary mentions mostly date back to early medieval Ireland and we don't know how ancient people celebrated it. The term appears in *Tochmarc Emire*, a tale in the Ulster Cycle, described as "when the ewes are milked at spring's beginning". Hutton writes of Imbolc: "It was placed in the Roman calendar, adopted by the Irish by the time that written records began, on 1 February."

Imbolc can involve thinking back to life in the past when most people were involved with agriculture, especially the lambing season at this time of year. But as a 21st century urban pagan I like to recognise what's relevant in my modern life. I might not be helping ewes give birth, but I can start working on new projects I want to see the light of day. I find this time is good to get creative with writing, crafting, and anything artistic. These can be done indoors without getting frozen on a hilltop.

Many pagans honour the goddess Brigid or Bride at Imbolc, while Catholics honour a Christian saint of the same name and possibly the same origin. Brigid is a goddess of many talents. She's associated with smithcraft, poetry – which I see as creative writing in general – and healing. She's also often connected with fire, which can mean light returning to the land, and water including sacred wells and springs. At Imbolc, or Imbolc Eve, an Irish custom is to make straw dolls called Bride dolls to display or parade in her honour. Brigid's crosses are woven out of rushes or straw and hung in windows for blessing and protection. February 2 is the Christian festival of Candlemas. It was traditionally celebrated by the blessing and lighting of candles for purification. Imbolc rituals can also involve lighting a candle to Brigid and asking for her blessing.

Floating Candle Magic

Here's one of my favourite spells. It uses floating candles and is intended to help your wishes and dreams come true[1]. You can work the magic alone or with friends. You need a floating candle for each person, a suitable bowl or cauldron of water and matches. Everyone should scratch their wish on their candle, light it and float it on the water. When all the candles are lit, visualise your wish coming true and chant three times:

Fire and water
Kindle and flow
Bring life to our dreams
And let them grow.

Magical Spring Cleaning

To make room for new energy in your life, it helps to clear out what you no longer need. Ideally spiritual cleansing comes after giving your home a physical tidy, but do what you feel capable of. Have a bath or shower to clean yourself, then clear your thoughts. Breathe in and out slowly several times. Visualise breathing out unwanted concerns and breathe in calmness and clarity. Open your windows at least a little to let out anything stale and let fresh air in.

Sweeping

A besom is a traditional witches' broom and is used to clear space. You can buy one or make your own with a bunch of twigs for the head and a pole for the handle. Birch twigs represent new beginnings. Pick some before the leaves start to grow. Ash can be used for the handle and represents magical power. Cut everything to the right size, bundle the twigs and tie them with twine, then insert the handle into the twig bundle and tighten it up more.

To ceremonially clean with a besom, sweep each room from the centre outwards in an anti-clockwise (widdershins) direction, and visualise unwanted energy being swept away. The anti-clockwise direction represents banishing.

Salt Water or Herbal Infusions

Salt is an ancient cleansing product. It kills bacteria, but has traditional uses in magical rites. Mix a pinch of salt into a bowl of clean water after visualising them being purified and dedicated for the task. Then sprinkle a little around each room.

Be careful not to get salty water on anything it could damage and make sure pets don't drink any.

You can use an infusion of cleansing herbs instead. One of my favourites is mugwort (sometimes called Artemisia), a protective herb which grows in England. A word of caution: mugwort shouldn't be used by anyone pregnant. Other herbs suitable for cleansing infusions include rosemary and lavender.

Smoke Cleansing
Many spiritual traditions use smoke to purify sacred space and these ceremonies have many names, but it's simplest to call it smoke cleansing. It can be done by burning dried herbs on their own, sticks of incense, or loose incense on a charcoal disk in an incense burner placed on a heat-proof surface. Again, mugwort, rosemary and lavender are suitable. Waft the smoke into corners, but make sure your room is well ventilated.

Light
Let sunlight or moonlight flood into your room and visualise it chasing away all unwanted energy. You can carry a candle lantern around, especially into dark corners where natural light doesn't reach. A safer alternative is to leave the candle on a flat surface and use a wand to visualise spreading light around you.

Bells and Gongs
Sound is another traditional way to clear unwanted energy. Go from room to room ringing a bell or striking a gong, again paying particular attention to murky corners.

Valentine's Day and Lupercalia
Valentine's Day on February 14 is, of course, massively commercialised with financial and social pressures. It isn't exactly a pagan love-fest as it gets its name from a Christian saint although many pagans point out the Ancient Roman

fertility festival of Lupercalia happened about the same time. It's actually more complicated. In mythology the founders of Rome, Romulus and Remus, were suckled as infants by Lupa the wolf. Lupercalia, on February 15, honoured her. A goat was sacrificed, a feast prepared, and strips of hide cut. Young men ran around the city with them, lightly whipping young women as a fertility custom. About the same time was the purification festival of Februa, honouring an aspect of the goddess Juno. The month of February is named after this[2]. Lupercalia and Februa got connected, but it was probably coincidence they happen about the same time as Valentine's Day.

In England, Valentine's Day was abolished as a Christian festival with the Reformation, but amorous customs grew despite that, so it's a secular tradition now. Valentine cards date to the 18th century, although gift-giving took place in the 17th century, mentioned by Samuel Pepys in his diaries. A folk belief is that birds choose mates on Valentine's Day, first mentioned by Chaucer in his 1382 poem The Parliament of Fowls. No one's certain he meant February 14, as calendars have changed and there's another Christian saint called Valentine[3]. However, birds do start to build nests in early spring, and people since ancient times would have seen that. Whatever the history, February is a good time for love spells to manifest your desires.

Heart-Shaped Vision Board for Self-Love Magic

Here's an easy crafting project to invite joy, love and good things into your life with a heart-shaped talisman. It uses the idea of vision boarding to help you attract what you want and focus on what makes you happy. Cut out a heart shape from cardboard, large enough to decorate. Then cut two identical shapes in coloured paper to glue over the front and back as a background for other images. Look for pictures of things you love and want to attract more of in your life. Photos, old greeting cards, wrapping paper, calendars or magazines can be sources. Cut pictures out and stick them on the heart using decoupage techniques. Paint diluted PVA glue on all sides of the paper to prime it. When that dries, use more PVA glue to stick the pieces in place. Draw or paint on the heart if you want then use coats of dilute PVA glue to varnish it. After you've created your talisman, meditate on it and visualise those things entering your life. Make a small hole at the top to put a loop of string to hang it where you will often see it, or put it on your altar.

Flower Lore

February also sees rapid change in my garden. At the start of the month I see some early flowers, including snowdrops, but by the end of it there'll be spring blossom everywhere.

Snowdrops

These are the quintessential flower of Imbolc and Candlemas. Their tiny white petals look so fragile but are hardy enough to survive snow. They're traditionally unlucky to bring indoors. According to *The Encyclopædia of Superstitions, Folklore, and the Occult Sciences of the World,* by Cora Linn Daniels, this belief arose because the white flowers look like tiny shrouds. Outdoors they're a sign of hope, so leave them where they are and enjoy them.

Crocuses

The flowers were sacred to the ancient Minoans – wall painting shows them being offered to a goddess. Ancient Egyptians believed crocuses granted visions. They included dried flowers in incense to identify thieves, according to Scott Cunningham in his *Encyclopedia of Magical Herbs.* The crocuses in my garden are yellow, which are one of the most common varieties. There are about eighty species of crocus, some of which are poisonous. The most valued is the edible saffron crocus, which has been used as dye and to flavour food for thousands of years. The saffron crocus originally came from ancient Mesopotamia but spread throughout the Mediterranean and further. Croydon, in South East England, originally meant "valley of the crocuses". However, the crocuses growing wild in the English countryside in spring are not the type used to make saffron. Leave them alone for everyone to enjoy.

Irises

Cloaked in a robe of dewdrops reflecting the stars, the Greek goddess Iris communicates messages via the rainbow between Heaven and Earth. The word iris means rainbow. In the language of flowers, the iris represents good news. Use the flowers in spells for communication. They can also help clear unwanted energy, so put some on your altar as part of spring cleaning.

Chapter 4

March, Spring and the Equinox

Named after Mars, the Roman god of war, March can bring stormy weather. However, for me, this is the first month of spring. There are many ways of noting the start of each season, as I mentioned in Chapter 1, and what's happening in nature is one of them. I ended the chapter on February with flowers and I'm continuing that theme. The sight of flowers lifts my mood when everything else seems grim, and this month is when my garden really starts to bloom with colour. It's March as I write this, and I can see yellow daffodils and pink primroses out of my window.

Flower Lore

Daffodils

The birthday flower for those born in March, daffodils are the national flower of Wales and worn on March 1 for St David's Day. They're also associated with the Spring Equinox. Magically, daffodils bring love, luck, and fertility. Put them on your altar when doing spells for those things or anywhere in your home for their bright yellow cheerfulness. Don't eat them, as they are poisonous. As an added precaution, avoid treading on daffs outside because gardening folklore says trampling them invites bad luck, whereas leaving them alone brings good luck. In Wales, a saying is that if you spot the first daffodil of the year you will find more gold than silver in the months to come.

Primroses

The name comes from the Latin *prima rosa*, meaning 'first rose' and they're steeped in folklore and magical custom. Primroses are a fairy flower. If they grow around your home they're said to protect those within. However, it's unlucky to bring them indoors[1]. They're also supposed to help people see fairies or things rendered invisible by them, and even open enchanted doorways by touching them with a posy[2].

Planting Seeds and Scarecrow Magic

March is when many types of seed are sown in my part of the world. Scarecrows are traditionally made to protect them. You could make a scarecrow as a guardian for anything you plant this spring – in the garden and in the sense of magical workings. Mini scarecrows can be created for window boxes or your altar. Here's a charm to say when making one:

Scarecrow, Scarecrow
Guard my seeds
Keep my plants
For me and the bees
Protect my loves
And wishes too
Scarecrow, Scarecrow
I count on you.

Lenten Times and Vegan Weeks

Lent is usually thought of as a Christian prelude to Easter, but it wasn't always just that. It might have originally derived from a word for the time of year when days lengthen, according to Professor Ronald Hutton in *The Stations of the Sun*, so it could be celebrated by anyone, pagans included. Hutton adds that historically it combined joy with abstinence. You don't have to be Christian to get into the Lenten spirit, which means enjoying warmth, light and the return of greenery while appreciating there isn't much fresh food in season – especially meat. In the past, a traditional Lent diet would have been largely vegan veg

29

and beans, even if the Church hadn't stipulated it. That idea can be revived by anyone wanting to reduce their meat and dairy consumption for ethical, environmental or spiritual reasons today, especially those working with the natural seasons. My own view is this is a better time for vegan weeks than January.

Equinox and Easter Connections

The Spring Equinox is usually on March 20, although it can be a day later or earlier. In the Wheel of the Year it's a time to celebrate springtime and all that means. That can include going outdoors to enjoy the sight of flowers blooming and buds forming, planting seeds (both real and metaphorical), and acknowledging the increasing light and warmth. It's also a festival associated with balance because it's when day and night are roughly equal length and is positioned between summer and winter. Both hemispheres of the Earth have the same amount of daylight, although it's Autumn Equinox in the southern hemisphere. The science is that the Earth is tilted on its axis. As it orbits the sun over the course of a year, the northern and southern hemispheres get more or less light, but at two points it illuminates both equally. These are the equinoxes and at those time the world is in balance.

The Christian festival of Easter falls on the first Sunday after the full moon following the Spring Equinox because Jesus's crucifixion is placed after Jewish Passover. Although Easter wasn't deliberately plonked on top of an ancient pagan festival, the reason it got the name is a little stranger, and possibly has some pagan origins. It often gets cited that the Venerable Bede, a monk in the early 8th century, wrote that the name derived from a goddess called Eostre. Although many modern pagans honour the goddess Eostre at this time, academics have debated whether the designation is accurate. Bede wasn't always correct and it's possible the Anglo-Saxon word 'eastre' was more to do with the season of spring itself rather than a specific goddess, or related to a goddess of the dawn like Eos instead of a goddess of that time of year.

Hutton writes that there isn't much evidence for a pre-Christian festival around the Spring Equinox. Nevertheless, while pre-Christian farmers might have been too busy sowing seeds to celebrate, it's possible older customs got lost or merged into Christian ones. We don't know, but that doesn't stop us creating modern-day pagan rituals full of the joys of springtime at the Equinox or over the Easter Bank Holiday.

Candle Ritual for Balance

This can be done at both equinoxes to help get more balance in life. You need two candles of different colours to represent day and night or summer and winter. Light the candles then sit down with your journal or a notebook and make two lists: one of things you want to make more time for in your life and the second of things you want to spend less time doing. As the candles burn further, visualise how you will manifest this in your life and ask the universe to help you. Keep the lists to remind yourself of your wishes.

Symbolism and Magic of Eggs

Many of us get eggs of some kind at Easter, even if we're pagan and don't celebrate it as a religious festival. For Christians, eggs are a symbol of rebirth at least as far back as the 4th century, when there are records of people presenting eggs at church to be blessed. According to Professor Ronald Hutton in a talk on spring customs to the Doreen Valiente Foundation[3] in 2021, the main reason people gave each other eggs at Easter historically was simply that there were lots of eggs around. It was a seasonal food in abundance and therefore enjoyed at the end of the Christian fast of Lent.

Eggs are symbols of birth, resurrection and creation in religions and cultures all over the world. In the mythologies of India, China, ancient Egypt and Ancient Greece, gods and goddesses – or indeed all of life itself – are said to be hatched from eggs. In alchemy, the egg has associations with the four elements. The shell represents earth, the membrane represents air, the white represents water and the yellow yolk represents fire. The philosopher's egg is the name of the crucible in which alchemists attempted to make the philosopher's stone.

In *An Egg at Easter: A Folklore Study* Venetia Newall speculates that primitive man must have seen birds hatching from the smooth ovoids that seemed otherwise like lifeless stones and thought magical forces were at work. The idea of the 'world egg' as the origin of the universe and the creator of life itself could have developed from this. As well as symbolising creation, eggs represent mystery. Venetia writes:

> There are so many strange conceptions about the egg: on the one hand it is pure and sacred and the bearer of radiant new life; on the other hand there is a secret inside, out of which anything may come to life: good and joyful, or bad.

This universal and ancient fascination with eggs makes them a powerful symbol, which you can use in spellwork and rituals. The magical properties of eggs include fertility, creation, life, new beginnings and divination. Divination with eggs is called oomancy. One way to do that is to drop the white into hot water and see what shape forms. If you don't like to waste food and aren't vegan, poach an egg for breakfast and have a look at the shape before serving.

Earth Hour and Honouring Gaia

Every year on a Saturday at the end of March is Earth Hour. People all over the world turn off electric lights for an hour to symbolise their commitment to the planet. Although organised by the World Wildlife Fund[4], it's a grassroots event and perfect to adopt for pagan ceremonies. Light a candle and make a dedication to do more for the environment. Do spells to protect wildlife and endangered habitats. Say words in honour of Gaia, Mother Nature, or any deity of protection for the Earth.

Chapter 5

April Fools to Walpurgis Night

April is one of those months without a modern pagan Wheel of the Year festival, but it begins with April Fool's Day. Here's a look at the origins of the day, the trickster and the wisdom of the fool. The idea of making fun of people on April 1 probably started in 1582 when Pope Gregory XIII's Gregorian Calendar replaced the Julian Calendar, meaning New Year's Day fell three months earlier. News travelled slowly then, and many people continued to celebrate the start of the year at the old time. They got called "April Fools". However, there are earlier references to April Fool type customs. Chaucer's story The Nun's Priest's Tale, written about 1400, is about two fools and takes place "thritty dayes and two" from the start of March, which would be April 1.

Tricksters and Wisdom

The trickster is an important figure in folklore, mythology, magic and divination. They appear in cultural traditions all over the world as deities, characters, spirits and animals. Tricksters include the Norse god Loki, the Greek goddess Eris, the Indigenous American Coyote and Raven, and Reynard the Fox from European folklore. They break the rules and use cunning to gain the upper hand. They can be serious troublemakers or humorous pranksters, bad guys or clowns, but we can learn lessons from them. In *Trickster Makes This World: Mischief, Myth and Art*, Lewis Hyde points out the trickster is one of the oldest mythological archetypes, dating back to the time of hunter gatherers, when trickery was often needed to catch food. He writes:

The trickster myth derives creative intelligence from appetite. It begins with a being whose main concern is being fed and ends with the same being grown mentally swift, adept at creating and unmasking deceit, proficient at masking his tracks and seeing through the devices used by others to mask theirs.

In today's world, creative problem solving is still important, but we're living in times when many people are trying to be more authentic in the way they present their identity. In *Pagan Portals – Loki, Trickster and Transformer*, Dagulf Loptson writes:

He will teach you to break the rules, live authentically, and never apologize for who you are...he will teach you...self-sufficiency, self-acceptance, creative problem solving, and marching to the beat of your own drum.

In tarot, the Magician, the first trump of the Major Arcana, follows the Fool, which is the zero card. The Magician is something of a performer and in some decks the card is called the Trickster. Essentially, the trickster is a guide or archetype for hard times, who teaches us to turn adversity to our advantage, to learn not only how to get out of trouble but also how to take advantage of it as if by magic. The trickster doesn't always win, but he gives himself a good chance of doing so.

Yet there's also value in the wisdom of the fool. In many tarot decks, the Fool card shows a carefree young person in colourful clothing enjoying a sunny walk along a cliff. They are setting out on a journey with a little dog at their heels, but possibly about to walk over the edge. The positive aspects of this card offer the lure of adventure, just as in April some of us might be looking forward to travel and holidays in the warmer weather. With the fun of being carefree, the message is to watch for dangers too. The little dog represents our natural intuition giving a warning.

The wisdom is to heed our instincts, and decide which risks are worth taking.

Festival of Cybele and Earth Day

Romans celebrated the festival of Megalesia from April 4 to 10. This was in honour of the Great Mother Cybele. She was earlier venerated by the Ancient Greeks and assimilated some of the attributes of Gaia, goddess of the Earth. She could be honoured early in April with libations and prayers, such as this one, from *Every Day Magic*:

> *Great Goddess, mountain-born Cybele*
> *Ancient Deity of Motherhood and Mystery*
> *My devotions I offer to you this day*
> *In the acts that I do and the words that I say...*

Cybele could also be called to on Earth Day, on April 22 each year, which raises awareness about the need to protect the planet. It started in 1970 but is now one of the biggest global environmental days of activity. Events you can take part in include webinars, litter clear-ups, and pledging sustainable action, but many pagans choose to perform rituals. Here's a chant you can use to empower Earth Day spells, inspired by dragon legends:

> *Earth Dragon*
> *Here my plea*
> *Earth Dragon*
> *Come to me*
>
> *Earth Dragon*
> *Guide my hand*
> *To protect*

This sacred land
Give me strength
And grant to me
Earth Dragon
Energy

At this time
Of spring's rebirth
Help me to
Restore our Earth

Earth Dragon
Hear my plea
Earth Dragon
Blessed be

Wildflower Lore

One way to help the environment is to encourage wildflowers in your garden. April gets its name from the Latin word *aperire*, which means 'to open'[1]. Here's a bit about two little flowers I see opening their petals in my lawn this month:

Dandelions

These are such useful plants it amazes me so many gardeners consider them weeds. You can eat the leaves in a salad, make a form of coffee from the roots, and infuse the petals as a tea which has a reputation for aiding divination work. St George's Day on April 23 is the traditional time to brew dandelion wine. Dandelions are a diuretic though, so check for any potential problems before drinking! Magically, they can be used in love spells, helping to transform problems, and general wish-making. Take a dandelion clock and make a wish. Then close your eyes and try to blow all the fluffy white seeds from the stalk in one go.

Daisies

Another wildflower I love to see brightening my lawn in April, daisies are associated with happiness, protection, courage and love, according to Rachel Patterson in *A Kitchen Witch's World of Magical Herbs & Plants*. She mentions the game where you pick a daisy and ask: "He loves me", then, "He loves me not" as you pluck petals, with the final one giving you the true answer to a question about love. You can extend that format for divination about anything. Say: "Daisy, give me your answer to my question." Pulling one petal off ask: "Should I do this?" Then ask: "Should I do that?" as you pluck the next. Do this slowly and visualise each of your options until the petals are gone. When you get to the last petal, you should have a possible answer. In the traditional game, whatever the last petal represents is correct but for this divination you should know the answer more correctly by how you feel about it. The flower is simply helping you tap into your own intuition. It's possible you'll know the answer the daisy gave is the right one, but if you have a strong feeling that answer isn't right for you at this time, trust your intuition.

Floralia and Walpurgis Night

As the natural wheel of the year turns smoothly, so does the transition between months. Some festivals straddle two. Floralia honours Flora, goddess of flowers and fertility. Under the Roman Empire the festival ran for six days starting April 28. People gave floral tributes and enjoyed games, theatre and dancing. Floralia might have been the inspiration for May Day fairs, but it's possibly coincidence as everyone wants to celebrate warmer weather, blossom and trees being green anew.

May Eve is magical but was considered a time when supernatural trouble-makers were about in a variety of traditions. In parts of Europe, especially Germany but also England, it's known as Walpurgis Night when witches were thought to gather and were historically seen as not the nice folk we are now. People would protect their homes against them. In Ireland it's more a time for fairies to do mischief. Mabh Savage, in *Every Day Magic*, writes about traditional May Eve protection for your home:

> *If the hawthorns are flowering near you, collect some May blossom, ideally before or at dawn, and hang it over your door. This will help protect you from the more mischievous of the Fae. If the blossom is yet to come, some hawthorn or rowan leaves will have the same effect. Ask the tree's permission, always say thank you and leave an offering if possible.*

Another May Eve protection custom is to put rowan crosses over doorways. Cross two rowan twigs and tie them together in the middle with red wool. Attach a loop to hang it. Lighting fires on May Eve is also a big tradition in a variety of places including Ireland, Scotland, the Isle of Man, and parts of England and Wales.

Springtime Guided Visualisation:
The Well in the Woods

This guided visualisation takes you into a wood in springtime to find a magical well where you will face choices about the future.

Sit comfortably and close your eyes. Take three deep breaths and relax. Visualise the following:

Visualise that you are in a beautiful place in the countryside on the edge of a wood, on a sunny spring morning. No other human is around. You feel safe, comfortable and at peace. You spot a path leading into the wood and decide to follow it. Make your way along the path, which winds through the trees. Above you is a fresh canopy of new green leaves. On the ground, either side of the path, are spring flowers. It's beautiful and peaceful. Visualise following the path through the wood. What do you see? What do you hear? What do you smell? Enjoy the sights and sounds and scents as you continue.

After a while, the path enters a grassy clearing dotted with wildflowers. In the centre of the clearing is a well. The well looks old and is surrounded by a low, circular wall. Four chalices stand on the edge of that wall. Enter the clearing and get closer. You see the chalices are empty. Look into the well. The water level is high. It smells fresh and looks cool and inviting. You realise you could reach it and take some with any of the chalices but, before you take any further action, you see the water surface shimmer. You hear a voice from within the well.

"I am the spirit of the well," they say. "This water offers many things, but only if you drink after choosing one of these cups. Look at each cup in turn, and I will tell you what magic it offers. You can only choose one cup to drink from."

You examine the first cup. The voice speaks: "If you draw water with this cup, it will give you the strength to make a difference in the world – to help, heal or do good for the planet. Study this cup, consider what you might do with this gift."

Look at the cup, examine it, and consider what it offers.

The voice speaks again and instructs you to look at a second cup. You do so, and the voice says: "If you draw water from the well and drink from this second cup, it will grant you a wish for something you personally desire. Think carefully about what you want, and what that might mean, before you drink, if you choose this cup."

Look at the second cup, examine it, and consider what it offers.

The voice then tells you to look at a third cup. You do so, and the voice says: "If you use this third cup to draw water, your thirst will be quenched and you will be refreshed, but that's all. Nothing else will change. Sometimes treading lightly on the Earth is the best course of action. Consider whether this is the cup you would drink from."

Look at the third cup, examine it, and consider what it offers. The voice then tells you to look at the fourth and final cup. You do so, and the voice says: "The fourth cup offers self-knowledge. This is of value to any who walk a spiritual path but be aware self-knowledge is not always comfortable. Consider whether this is the cup you would drink from."

Look at the fourth cup, examine it, and consider what it offers. The voice says: "Now, if you would drink from the well, choose a cup to draw water, and the gift it offers."

Make your final decision – whether to drink from the first cup, of strength to make a difference in the world; the second cup, for something you desire; the third cup, offering only refreshment; or the fourth and final cup, offering self-knowledge. You have a fifth choice, of course, to drink from none. Once you've made your decision, take the cup, dip it into the well, fill it with water and drink if you wish.

The water is pure, cool and refreshing. As you finish drinking, or if you chose not to drink, the cup in your hand vanishes, as do all the others. The voice speaks again. "You made your choice. Remember whatever choices and actions we make in life affect what happens in the future. Even inaction can affect what happens. Change is not always obvious, and it can be slow, but what we do or don't do can make a difference."

The voice finishes and you sense the presence no more. The well is still there, with its low wall, in this grassy clearing in the wood, but the water no longer shimmers, and you hear only the natural sounds of the wood around you. Yet you feel the choice you made will be important.

Retreat from the glade and return along the path through the wood. You safely reach the edge of the wood and look around once more at the beautiful countryside on this spring morning. It's now time to return to your normal reality.

When you are ready, take a deep breath, shake your fingers and toes, and open your eyes to the real world.

Think more about what choice you made in the visualisation and what that might mean to you. Make notes in your journal or sketch pictures of what you visualised.

Chapter 6

May and Summer Is Icumen In

May begins with Beltane in the modern pagan Wheel of the Year. It's time to celebrate the joys of life and love. All around is greenery and blossom; birds are nesting and bees are dancing. Spring is in its final flowering and "Summer is Icumen In", as the song goes. The name Beltane originates in an ancient Irish festival. The early Irish text *Sanas Cormaic* reveals it means 'lucky fire' and goes on to say two huge fires were lit at the start of summer. Druids would bless them, and cattle driven between them to ward off diseases. A fire festival called 'Beltine' at the start of summer is also mentioned in the tale of the wooing of Emer, *Tochmarc Emire*.

May Day, Queens and Jack-in-the-Green

The English concept of 'Maying' – of celebrating May Day by wearing flower garlands and decking homes with hawthorn blossom as well as partying, is a bit different from Beltane. Steve Roud, in *The English Year*, writes: "Judging by the range of traditional customs that took place on May Day, it was second only to Christmas in popularity with the English People." It's mentioned in medieval English literature, including that of Chaucer, who wrote about the maypole in the poem Chaunce of the Dice. According to Professor Ronald Hutton in *The Stations of the Sun*, Gaelic regions tended to have fire ceremonies while in southern England poles were customary. Despite Sir James Frazer, in *The Golden Bough*, suggesting maypoles were the remnants of ancient tree-spirit worship, or ideas they were phallic, Hutton writes that they were more likely "useful frameworks upon which garlands...could be hung, to form a focal point for celebration [of]...the returning strength of vegetation."

In recent history, two archetypal figures have been celebrated on May Day in England – the May Queen and Jack-in-the-Green. May Queens presided over festivities, awarded prizes and led processions. When I was a child, May Queens were chosen in beauty pageants that tended to be ableist, sizeist, ageist and racist. Few in my multi-cultural, working-class London suburb were of the physical type likely to win the crown. I'd have had more hope as a Wednesday Addams lookalike, so I never entered the contest. Since then I've learnt the image of the May Queen dressed in white – and probably with blond hair and blue eyes – is recent. Roud writes: "The May Queen is so much part of England's accepted May Day iconography that we assume it to be an ancient institution, but it is, in fact, almost entirely another nineteenth century invention." It comes from things like Tennyson's poem The May Queen and Washington Irving's *Sketch-Book*.

While many Victorians envisaged the May Queen as a symbol of virtue and purity, now it's common for pagans to view her as the leader of sexually charged Beltane revels, a symbol of fertility, desire and sensuality at a time when nature is all about the birds and the bees and the drive to reproduce. However, Hutton points out that historically England was too cold in early May for outdoor sex. In fact, the registers of births from bygone times indicate people kept their pants on until later. There's even an old saying, which might be about the month or the flower: "Button to chin, till May be in, cast not a clout, till May be out." Nevertheless, for modern pagans, the May Queen can be ritualised as an aspect of a more mythical figure or goddess, perhaps Flora. Any who feel the call can welcome the spirit of the May Queen into their hearts, take the hand of their beloved and dance the summer in. But the Goddess can reappear and reinvent herself, and May Queens can be any age, shape or appearance too.

The foliage-clad figure of Jack-in-the-Green, accompanied by musicians and people in fancy dress, is also a familiar May Day sight in English towns. He resembles the Green Man, epitomised by foliate heads carved in many medieval churches and thought by some to be a relic of pre-Christian nature worship. However, there are many other interpretations which are more typical of medieval Christian viewpoints, according to Hutton in *Queens of the Wild*. Similarities in appearance aside, the current theory is Jack-in-the-Green customs began no earlier than the 17th century, independently of other folklore. Dairy maids and chimney sweeps took to the streets carrying the utensils of their trades decorated with garlands to raise money. The garlands grew and the sweeps were transformed into Jack covered in greenery. Whatever the true origins, it's hard to see Jack-in-the-Green celebrations today without feeling you're witnessing something wild and pagan. The God and Goddess can both reinvent themselves.

These strands from myth and history can merge into a modern festival to celebrate fertility or the joys of life. You can celebrate the traditional fire festival, but if a bonfire isn't practical you can light a candle and visualise its flame as your own Beltane blaze. You can make flower garlands. You can dress as a May Queen or Jack-in-the-Green – or make poppets to represent them, dress them in miniature garlands and put them on your altar. You can erect a maypole, deck the halls with hawthorn, or explore other May Day customs as you desire. You don't have to celebrate on May 1. If the hawthorn isn't in bloom, you can wait or adapt to what's going on in nature.

A Solitary Beltane Celebration

To me, May 1 feels like a day to do something special, even if it's not a holiday. If you're at work or rushing with weekday chores, allow yourself a break. You could take a packed lunch to the park or garden and appreciate the greenery. After you've relaxed in the open air, think what you like about yourself that doesn't involve helping others. This can be hard to do, but here's one way:

- Make a list of at least three things you enjoy doing.
- Next to each write that you love the attribute which enables you to do that activity. For example, if you love dancing, next to that write "I love that I can dance", if you love reading, write "I love being able to read".
- Write at the bottom of your list: "I love the fact that I am alive!" Because Beltane is a day to love being alive.

Don't worry about what other people think, this is about what you love doing. My mum was partially deaf since early childhood and unable to sing in tune yet she loved to sing and often did. She would say, "I have a song in my heart. It doesn't matter if other people can recognise it." It would be fine to write: "I love that I have a song in my heart."

A Bubbly Spell for Happiness
Go outside with bubble mixture on a sunny day. Picture in your mind something that fills you with joy and delight. Imagine sending those happy thoughts into bubbles as you blow them. Do this with as many joyful images as you can think of. As each bubble bursts, happiness is released into the world, where it will grow. More happiness will return to you in your own life as a result[1]. This is a spell you can do any time, but is appropriate for the energy of May.

Wildflowers, Magic and Eco-Paganism

Paganism is often called a nature religion, so caring for nature is a sacred task as well as protecting the world for the future. I believe in acting locally and you can't get much more local than your own garden. No Mow May is a campaign by conservation charity Plantlife[2] to let lawns grow this month so wildflowers can flourish as food for bees, butterflies and other insects. According to its Every Flower Counts (EFC) survey:

A one metre square on a typical EFC lawn last year had 17 daisies and a smattering of buttercups and dandelions. Across lawns, germander speedwell and field forget-me-nots were next most likely to show. Such a square of lawn would produce about two milligrams of nectar sugar and three microlitres of pollen per day.

Here's more about the folklore and magic of wildflowers you might find if you let your lawn grow in May:

Buttercups
I'm sure we all remember an old game with these bright yellow flowers – hold one under your chin to see if you like butter. Honestly, I think tasting butter is a more direct method than floral divination! In spellcraft they're associated with wealth and protection as well as fortune telling.

Germander Speedwells
These little blue flowers traditionally bestow good luck on travellers as the sight of them is said to speed people on their way. A sprig can be worn as a charm when embarking on a journey. Bees will love them too as they buzz around your garden.

Forget-me-Nots
Meaning true love according to *The Language of Flowers* by Margaret Pickston, they can be used in fidelity spells. If you wear one, ideally in a hat, it's supposed to help you see past illusions, particularly those caused by fairies[3].

Bluebells
It's considered unlucky to bring this quintessential early May flower indoors. Folklore suggests even trampling them outside invites bad luck. However, they do present an environmental

quandary. In England there are native bluebells and non-native Spanish ones. Crossbreeding means the British plants are dying out. Bluebells have grown in my garden since I was a child, and at one time they were the native type. Over the years they've become hybridised. I could weed out my hybrids, but in London most bluebells are like mine. If I replanted native ones, they would quickly hybridise again. So, I let my bluebells grow tall for luck and because I love them.

The Ides of May, Maia, and Oak Apple Day

May 15 is the Ides of May. On this day the Vestal Virgins of Ancient Rome performed a rite to ensure the water supply. Part of the ceremony involved throwing 24 doll-like mannikins into the River Tiber. These were small effigies made of straw, which may have replaced earlier human sacrifice. These days I wouldn't recommend throwing anything into a river that might cause pollution or blockage, but you could cut 24 person shapes out of something ducks could eat, such as lettuce leaves. Use a gingerbread person cookie cutter as a template, then go to your local waterway that allows duck feeding. With climate change meaning more years of drought or flood, as well as plastic in our seas and rivers, this could be incorporated into a modern pagan rite to protect our waters. It would also be an auspicious time to think of ways to conserve more water or take part in a beach or river bank clean-up.

Mercury, Roman god of commerce, was also honoured on the Ides of May. The name for month of May is possibly derived from the mythological figure Maia[4]. She was a nymph companion of the Greek goddess Artemis, and also the mother of Hermes who the Romans named Mercury.

If it didn't feel seasonally right to celebrate Beltane at the start of the month, there's another chance to wear garlands of flowers on May 29. This is Oak Apple Day, or Restoration Day, and was once a popular public holiday in England to commemorate the restoration of the monarchy in May 1660. The garlands traditionally included oak leaves and oak apples, which are a type of plant gall, honouring the legend that King Charles II escaped the Roundheads by hiding in an oak tree after the Battle of Worcester in 1651.

Chapter 7

June, Solstice and Midsummer

The days are warm and at their longest, so visiting sacred sites for a huge celebration is a glorious thing to do. This is probably why the big Wheel of the Year festival for many pagans is the Summer Solstice. There are also other things to celebrate or commemorate this month, including the Roman Queen of Heaven herself, Juno[1], who the month is named after.

Ancestors of Tradition, Father's Day, Goddess Days and Eco Festivals

Some of the most influential figures of the modern pagan revival were born in June. Alex Sanders, who founded the Alexandrian tradition of Wicca and was called the King of the Witches, was born on June 6, 1926. Gerald Brosseau Gardner is considered the father of the modern Wiccan movement. He was born on June 13, 1884. William Butler Yeats, who was a member of the Hermetic Order of the Golden Dawn and whose poetry was inspired by Irish mythology, was also born on June 13, in 1865. Ross Nichols, who founded the Order of Bards, Ovates and Druids, was born on June 28, 1902.

People in the UK, US and many parts of the world celebrate Father's Day on the third Sunday in June. This began in the early 1900s and gained international recognition due to the work of a US woman, Sonora Smart Dodd. It would a good time to remember male ancestors of tradition, such as Gardner, Sanders, and Nichols. Although it's primarily a secular festival, on Father's Day you could choose to honour father gods such as Odin the All-Father from Norse mythology.

Several June festivals are associated with Ancient Roman goddesses. The first day, or Kalends, of June is the festival of

Carna, goddess of the heart who protects from vampiric attacks, and Cardea, her fellow goddess of hinges and doors. Cleanse the entrance to your home, oil hinges, and hang a protective charm above your front door[2]. June 9 to 15 was a festival for Vesta, goddess of the hearth and home. People would visit her temple with bread and flowers, and it was then ritually cleansed. Celebrate by baking bread, making an offering to Vesta then cleaning your kitchen and sacred spaces. The goddess Fortuna was honoured on June 24 with drinking, merrymaking and playing games. Similar festivities could be done today.

Modern annual events this month focus on the environment. June 5 is World Environment Day, June 8 is World Oceans Day, and June 18 is an international day for combatting drought. As well as taking part in official activities on these days, we can try to reduce the impact of our own pagan festivals on the environment. Celebrate close to home or use public transport rather than cars to get to events, avoid single-use plastic at picnics, dispose of waste responsibly and help with general site clear-ups.

Summer Solstice

Honouring the sun at its height, we can hope to get outdoors and celebrate the longest day of the year with everything from solemn ritual to wild partying. The date of the longest day can vary between June 20 to 22 from year to year. The word Solstice comes from the Latin *sol sistere*, which means 'sun stand still'. The Earth doesn't actually stop moving around our sun, but the moment of the solstice, when we switch from lengthening days to shortening days, seems spiritually like a moment of stillness to contemplate the turning of the year. You'll sometimes see it given the name Litha as the Anglo-Saxon historian Bede wrote that Litha was a Saxon word for this time of year. Modern pagans, especially Wiccans, adopted the name for the summer Wheel of the Year festival. A Druid name for the festival is Alban Hefin, which means 'the light of summer'.

Whatever we call it now, the Summer Solstice has been marked as a special occasion for thousands of years and by many cultures. Fire was a big part of many historic celebrations, including bonfires, torchlit processions and sometimes rolling burning wheels down hills. Professor Ronald Hutton, in *The Stations of the Sun*, writes that mid to late June was a popular time for festivities of this kind in many parts of Europe. The fires were often seen as a form of purification and to ward off evil, but probably also symbolised the fire of the sun. A burning wheel is a common sun symbol. Hutton believes there's enough evidence to suggest midsummer fire festivals stretch back to ancient pagan times. He writes: "The dossier seems to be complete enough to speak confidently of a pre-Christian seasonal ritual of major importance."

Modern celebrations have to take fire safety more seriously than our ancestors did, but you could light outdoor fires where they're allowed. Indoors you can use candles. Candle vigils are a lovely way to celebrate Solstice Eve. Watch the sun go down and light a candle in a lantern as the last rays leave the sky. Sit a vigil and watch the longest day dawn, but don't stare at the sun as it can cause eye damage. You could create sun symbols from natural materials without setting them alight. There are examples of equal-armed crosses in a circle from very ancient times, but modern pagan variants sometimes give them eight equal arms to represent the Wheel of the Year itself. Another popular solar symbol is a sunburst or a circle with rays. You don't have to stick precisely to ancient traditions, but you could use those ideas if you're creating seasonal mandalas as I suggested in Chapter 1.

Many pagans – as well as spiritual tourists – like to travel to famous ancient sacred sites such as Stonehenge to watch the sunset on Solstice Eve or the sunrise at dawn, but you can have a more personal experience with less travel close to home. I sometimes climb a local hill to greet the sunrise. Research

St John's Wort

Historically, St John's Day, on June 24, was when it was customary to gather St John's wort. This herb with yellow flowers has long been used to keep evil away magically and as well as in medicine. It's still sometimes used to treat depression today, although I'm not offering medical advice. From at least medieval times the herb has been hung over doors and windows to keep away malefic spirits and spellcasters. In some areas, the flowers were traditionally dipped in a bowl of water and left outside exposed overnight to create a beauty potion in which to wash one's face. Rachel Patterson, in *A Kitchen Witch's World of Magical Herbs and Plants* writes that St John's wort is useful in love divination magic and in truth spells.

Honeysuckle

Although many types of honeysuckle flower all year, the one in my garden blooms prolifically in June. Honeysuckle growing near your home is said to attract money, love, and luck, as well as offer protection. Its sweet scent is also supposed to help clear the mind and promote psychic powers. Magically, it can be used in spells for abundance. You can put dried honeysuckle flowers in incense blends, pouches, and poppets. The flowers can be used for sweetening spells to help with relationships, but the vines can be used for binding too. Don't eat the berries as many varieties are poisonous to humans.

Wild Roses

While cultivated roses flower all summer, wild roses only flower once. The ones in my garden have pale pink blooms with five petals as well as sharp thorns along the stems. Although all roses symbolise love, the wild rose also symbolises the wildness of nature, which can be both beautiful and cruel. They often need cutting back if you don't want a home like Sleeping Beauty's castle. Pruned rose stems can be transformed into wands. Dry them, cut them to length, and sand or cut off thorns at the handle end. Rose wands can be used in love magic, but also for cutting unwanted romantic ties and dispelling enchantment. The rose is sacred to both Aphrodite and Isis. The rose of Isis appears in the allegorical novel *The Golden Ass* as "the sweet Rose of reason and virtue" that saves the hero from a bewitched life as a donkey. A rose wand can be used for magic you don't want discovered. In Ancient Rome the wild rose was the symbol for secrets, associated with Harpocrates, god of silence and confidentiality. Romans placed a wild rose on doors or painted them around ceilings of rooms where confidential matters were discussed. The phrase *sub rosa*, or 'under the rose', means to keep a secret.

Chapter 8

July's Dog Days and Summer Fairs

July is the start of the Dog Days of Summer, which run through to August. It doesn't have anything to do with puppies, but relates to when Sirius, the Dog Star, rises in the sky at dawn. That varies a bit from country to country. The Dog Days supposedly mark the hottest of the year. The name comes from an ancient belief that Sirius, which is the brightest star in the constellation Canis Major, brought hot weather. Although the star doesn't actually affect the weather, it often appears during the sultriest days and the term's still used for them.

For Ancient Egyptians, Sirius first appeared before the annual Nile flood, which was vital for agriculture. Farmers would watch for an indicator that the flood was due. Although the Egyptians looked forward to the Dog Days, many other cultures considered them to be a time of ill-omen. Brady's *Clavis Calendaria*, or a compendious analysis of the calendar, published in 1813, describes the Dog Days as an evil time "when the seas boiled, wine turned sour, Quinto raged in anger, dogs grew mad, and all creatures became languid, causing to man burning fevers, hysterics, and phrensies." A traditional English folk saying implies the Dog Days can either be a good or bad sign depending on the weather:

Dog Days bright and clear
indicate a happy year.
But when accompanied by rain,
for better times our hopes are vain.

Customs and Festivals
There were traditionally many July fairs in England – some still happen. Steve Roud in *The English Year* mentions Farlop

Fair taking place by an oak tree in Epping Forest in early July. Stagshawbank Fair was on July 4 at Corbridge, Northumberland. Old Midsummer's Day falls on July 5 and many festivals marked it, often with bonfires. On July 6, Kilburn Feast, in North Yorkshire, was a massive horse fair. On the first Saturday in July it was traditional to change the rushes once common as household floor coverings. Rush bearing ceremonies involved carrying rushes and flowers around the village in a parade, often woven into symbolic shapes. The whole thing was like a carnival.

The month gets its name from Julius Caesar[1], who was named as a god after his death but is probably little worshipped today. A deity perhaps more appealing to honour in July is Concordia, Roman goddess of concord or peace. The festival of Lucaria on July 21 is sacred to her[2]. On July 25 is the Ebernoe Horn Fair, in West Sussex. Horn fairs occur in various parts of England and their origins aren't entirely known. Some may date back to ancient pagan times, but it isn't clear through historical records. In Ebernoe a sheep is roasted and cricket played. The winning team is given the sheep's horns, while everyone can enjoy a feast of roast lamb.

Herb Lore

In England, July's a wonderful month for enjoying the sights and scents in gardens. You can make the most of floral abundance to collect petals and leaves to dry. Tie them in bundles and hang them upside down from a drying rack in a well-aired place, away from sunlight or direct heat. Putting them in a paper bag will prevent bits dropping off. Alternatively, collect the dried petals that fall from flowers in vases. When they're completely dry, store them in airtight jars out of sunlight to use in incense blends, poppets, pouches, jar spells or other magic. Here are a few of July's magical blooms:

Pot Marigolds

These sun-loving flowers with beautiful burnt-orange blooms are magically associated with psychic powers, luck, and happiness. A vase of marigolds in your home helps attract good luck and is said to lift the spirits of all who dwell there.

Chamomile

One of the most popular herbal teas or infusions, chamomile is often drunk for relaxation. According to Rachel Patterson in *A Kitchen Witch's World of Magical Plants and Herbs*, chamomile tea can be used in spells to attract money by washing your coins in it or sprinkling it over your notes. I guess you could wash your credit card too.

Echinacea

Many believe echinacea may help stave off colds, but the flowers can be used in healing spells too and this book is about magical information rather than anything medical. Put a vase of the flowers on your altar when doing healing magic. It can also be used to strengthen the effects of other herbs in spells.

Lavender

As well as having a wonderful perfume, lavender is one of the most useful plants a witch can grow. The name comes from the Latin *lavare*, meaning to wash. The Romans liked to bathe in lavender-scented water, and you can use lavender-infused water for magical cleansing too. The smoke from burning the herb is also cleansing. Bags of dried flowers have traditionally been hung in wardrobes to deter moths and put in pillowcases to aid sleep. Magically, it can help with divinatory dreams and boost psychic powers. It's a good ingredient in love spells. To communicate with a loved one, perhaps to try to resolve a problem, write them a letter on lavender scented paper as it's associated with forgiveness and romance.

Hollyhocks

Hollyhocks are a traditional English summer sight, with tall stalks and huge bell-shaped blooms. In the language of flowers, they're a symbol of fertility and fruitfulness because they produce hundreds of seeds. Put a flower or two on seasonal altars, but leave plenty in the garden as bees, butterflies, and moth caterpillars love them. They're also associated with fairy magic. A recipe of 1660 describes a potion to enable you to see fairies made from hollyhock buds mixed with marigolds, wild thyme, and young hazel buds.

Mint

July is perfect to pick fresh mint leaves. As well as putting them in tea, cocktails, and cooking in general, magically their powers include healing, protection, and use in money spells. Grow a pot of mint near your home, wash your piggy bank with mint infusion, or keep a leaf in your purse or wallet.

Peace Dust Spell

This lovely spell using dried flowers was devised by my fellow witch Jane Mortimer and I'm glad she's given me permission to share it. You need dried petals from any flowers with peaceful associations. Jane said: "I snipped off a bowl full of tired-looking roses, pelargoniums and scented geraniums, plus a few of their leaves, some violet leaves, feverfew, and stems of wheat that grew from the bird food. All these botanicals are ruled by Venus, but I added quite a bit of spearmint, ruled by Mercury, because the scents go so well together, and Mercury could help speed things up."

Sprinkle the lot with a splash of ylang ylang essential oil and add a handful of green cardamon pods. Hang this up in a paper bag to dry for a week, then cut out the main rose stems and put everything else in a food chopper. Jane said: "A pestle and mortar doesn't cut it with this lot, trust me!"

Fill a jar with Peace Dust and use it to make home protection spells, saying: "Vile intent from other mortal, enter not across this portal." The dust can be sprinkled across the front doorway to stop people bringing malevolence into the home. It can also be used as incense or pot pourri.

Summer Guided Visualisation:
The Wise Woman's Cottage

This will take you on a journey through lanes and fields to visit a wise woman for wisdom and divination. The original version of this is in my earlier book *Pagan Portals – Guided Visualisations*, but as it's one of my favourites I am sharing it here too.

Sit comfortably and close your eyes. Take three deep breaths in and out and relax, then visualise the following:

Visualise you are in a baker's shop, in a small village in the countryside. It's a beautiful, warm summer's day. You've been asked to deliver a basket of freshly baked bread to an old woman who lives on her own in a cottage on edge of the village, beyond the first field.

Taking the basket, you go through the baker's shop door onto the village street of old cottages, with gardens full of flowers. You pass through the village. At the end of the street is a fence with a stile and beyond that a field full of ripe crops. Cross the stile and enter the field. A path leads around the edge and you see poppies and other wildflowers and herbs growing in the borders. Looking into the field, you see in the distance the crop being harvested under the hot sun. Above you birds soar in the sky. Perhaps you catch a glimpse of other animals too. Observe what's happening as you travel along the path.

At the far end of the field is an old hedge. After a while your reach it. In the hedge is a gate. This leads into the old woman's garden behind her cottage. Open the gate and walk into the garden, closing the gate behind you.

The garden at first seems overgrown, with trees at the sides, shrubs and bushes and tall plants offering dappled shade. Make your way further into the garden, where bright flowers grow everywhere. Bees are going from flower to flower and butterflies flit among them.

You see the old woman. She's harvesting berries and putting them into a basket. Go to her and greet her. She smiles and greets you in reply, then invites you into her cottage. She opens the door and you follow her inside. Look around, what do you see there?

The old woman invites you to sit at her table and put down the basket of bread, then she offers you tea. She prepares the tea using leaves in an earthenware teapot and brings out a jar of fresh jam she has made from fruit from her garden, with butter and milk she tells you are from a neighbour's farm.

You join her for tea. The fresh bread, jam and other produce are delicious. You talk with her as you enjoy your tea together. What do you talk about?

When you have finished your tea, she asks if you would like her to divine your future or answer a question, by reading the patterns in the leaves at the bottom of the cup. If you do, let her see the cup.

She turns it three times clockwise then holds it to the sunlight streaming through the cottage window. Then she answers your question and reveals what the future might possibly hold for you. If you want, she can show you the patterns in the leaves and how she interpreted them.

Now it's time for you to leave. Pick up the empty bread basket and say goodbye. As you are about to go, the old woman puts a final gift for you into the basket. Look at it and thank her, then go out of the cottage door.

You go back through her garden, through the gate in the hedge, along the path at the edge of the field and over the stile into the village. After passing along the street, you return the basket to the bakery shop, where you began your journey. You may keep the gift the old woman gave you and remember what she said.

When you are ready, shake your arms and legs and open your eyes to the real world.

Feasting and Tealeaf Reading

After that visualisation you could have a harvest feast, or just fresh bread and jam and a cup of tea. You could also try tealeaf reading. Use loose-leaf tea and don't strain it. When you have finished drinking, swirl the remains around the cup three times and upend it into the saucer to drain off excess liquid. Turn the cup back the right way and look inside for symbols or shapes. Use your intuition to divine meanings.

Chapter 9

August Harvests and Holidays

This month traditionally sees the start of the grain harvest; historically time for a big celebration, as people relied on each year's crops for food to last through winter. These days it's more a time for holidays. The month is named after Augustus Caesar[1], the first Roman emperor, who also liked to visit foreign countries, but mainly to conquer them. Apparently, this was the month when most of the conquering happened.

Lammas, Lughnasadh and Celebrating Achievements

One name for the festival of the first fruits is Lammas. It was once the time for summer fairs where workers were hired to bring in the harvest, livestock was sold, and everyone had a good time. The word might come from the Anglo-Saxon *'hlafmaesse'*, meaning loaf mass. Ninth century records show loaves baked from the first grains being blessed then, according to Steve Roud in *The English Year*. These days Lammas is a name used for the Pagan Wheel of the Year festival on August 1 and is also celebrated in Traditional Witchcraft. In *Crone! – An Old Craft Witch's Year*, Melusine Draco writes:

> *Lammas is a most important Old Craft festival… Originally it was held on 1st August, or about halfway between the Summer Solstice and Autumn Equinox.*

Some prefer to call the festival Lughnasadh, after the Irish god Lugh. Lughnasadh remembers the funeral Lugh held for his foster-mother, Tailtiu, who legends say died after clearing Ireland's plains for agriculture. A good way to celebrate the grain harvest is to bake your own bread. Fresh bread is perfect to share at a Lammas ritual or as a treat to honour the season. Enjoy the lovely loaf, then sprinkle a few crumbs onto the ground outside and give thanks to nature for her bounty.

Grain is also essential for brewing beer, and that's something to celebrate too. John Barleycorn is a folk song often sung at modern pagan Lammas rites. It's about a character who is the personification of barley and shows the process grain goes through from harvest to raising a glass as a toast. There are many versions of the song, but it usually starts with the grain cut down, which can be thought of as a symbolic sacrifice, and ends with it resurrected as beer. Beer is traditionally shared at Lammas rites along with bread. Raise a toast to John Barleycorn and any other deities you honour, then sprinkle a little as an outdoor libation.

Modern urban pagans might not have grain to harvest, but we can celebrate veg or flowers we've grown and personal achievements such as exam results, business success, a lifestyle goal, or completed project. Create an altar using things symbolising the harvest and high summer. Place on it items that reflect anything you feel proud of or are grateful for. Light an orange or gold candle and say words of thanks, perhaps followed by a harvest feast or a party.

Corn Dollies

Corn dollies made from stalks of wheat or other grain are associated with harvest time, although they only got that name about 100 years ago according to Roud in *The English Year*. He writes that the custom of making figures from grain stalks or straw goes back to at least the 16th century, but the term 'corn dolly' was invented in the early 20th century by country artisans "who developed straw-work in a…complex craft" as decorative objects. Before that straw figures were more often called kern, kirn or churn babies. There's a lot of folklore associated with them. While in some traditions the first sheaf of wheat was baked into bread, in others it was made into something to be burnt as a symbolic thank-you.

Some corn dollies look human-shaped, but often they're more stylised and look nothing like a person. One example is a countryman's favour or lover's knot, often given as love tokens at harvest time and simple to make. The easiest is a plait of grain stalks tied into a loop. Corn dollies or favours can be made with long, thick strands of grass from your garden or with craft straws as well as real grain stalks. Never pick crops from fields unless you have the farmer's permission.

Straw or grain figures are also made at the end of the harvest. According to Sir James Frazer in *The Golden Bough* the last sheaf of the harvest was made into a corn dolly with a hollow enclosure for the grain spirit to live in during winter. In spring, it would be ploughed into the first furrow of the field to return the spirit to the land. That might be a romanticised idea. In parts of Scotland and some Scandinavian countries, straw dogs known as 'bikko' are made as booby prizes given to the last farmer to bring in their crops. The bikko is traditionally made from the last sheaf, or straw, and secretly attached to the roof of the recipient's house during the night. It's considered a sign of bad luck rather than a favour or a home for a spirit.

Fruit and Herb Lore

August is a great month for blackberrying and other foraging. I live in a London suburb, but find all sorts of wildflowers and fruit in overgrown alleyways. Obviously don't go picking things from parks or other people's gardens or fields without permission, don't take more than you need, don't pick rare plants or herbs, and leave plenty for wildlife. Also check whether any herbicides have been sprayed there.

Blackberries

According to Manx folklore, the first berries of the season should be left for the fairies. If you ignore this advice, the saying is that others you pick will be full of grubs. Folklore also says you shouldn't pick blackberries after St Michaelmas Day, September 29. According to Christian mythology, that's supposed to be the anniversary of when Lucifer was chucked out of heaven, landing in a bramble bush. He likes to mark the occasion by peeing over everyone's brambles. Whatever the truth of those tales, the sweetest, juiciest blackberries are found from mid-August to early September.

Poppies
There are hundreds of different poppy types. The Class A drug opium is extracted from the opium poppy although others have uses in spells for sleep, love matters, inducing forgetfulness and easing suffering. August is a great month for collecting seeds for spellwork, including poppies. Shake the head on a dry day. If it rattles, the seeds are ready. Seeds work well in poppets and jar magic. There's more poppy lore in the chapter on November.

Hawthorn Berries
While hawthorn blossom was used for protection in May, you can now use the berries for protection magic. The dried berries are also great for putting into poppets to represent the heart, and in spells for matters of love.

Celebrating Cats and the Goddess Diana
While we might still be in the Dog Days of summer, this month also holds modern-day cat festivals. International Cat Day takes place on August 8 to raise awareness for our feline companions. Events are organised by International Cat Care[2], a not-for-profit organisation. Spend quality time with your cat if you have one. You can sit and meditate with your moggie. If your cat likes being stroked, do that mindfully, be in the moment and let other worries and concerns slip away. Black Cat Appreciation Day is on August 17 in the US, although it's different in the UK, where National Black Cat Day is on October 27 and run by Cats

Protection[3] with the aim of promoting the beauty of black cats. As a witch, I don't think you can celebrate black cats too often so why not do both?

In ancient Rome, August 13 was the start of Nemoralia, or Festival of Torches, a three-day celebration of Diana, goddess of women, children, animals, hunting and the moon. It was a time of rest and celebration, especially for women. Those participating would bathe, beautify themselves, and process by torchlight around the shores of Lake Nemi, which was sacred to Diana, under the moon. Worshippers offered fruit, asked for her blessings, and danced. Diana is a goddess much revered by modern witches as a symbol of feminine strength. The concept of the huntress can be applied to pursuing a goal or tracking down an object of desire. Personally, I see her as being a goddess of photographers too, as there's as much skill needed in getting a great shot of an animal with a camera as there is in hunting one. Here's a prayer to her:

Lady of the Moon
Diana, virgin huntress
Protector of the innocent
I call upon you and ask you
to give me your blessings
and help me find my way.

Holiday Magic

August is peak holiday time. If you're a city pagan, it can be a much-needed opportunity to visit wilder places and feel more in touch with nature. However, it can sometimes be hard to fully relax into the holiday mood. If you're away at the coast, let the salt water of the sea wash away your worries with a sea purification. This is best done on an ebbing tide as you can imagine all your concerns being carried away. At the sea shore, let the waves wash over your feet and tell the water your woes. Say:

Great Mother Sea,
Carry my fears
away from me.

After you've finished, thank the goddess of the water and offer in return to help her by clearing litter from the beach. In particular, pick up plastic rubbish because it's not biodegradable and harms marine life. Put it in a recycling bin.

In England the month ends with a bank holiday, which I think of as summer's last hurrah. Marldon, in Devon, holds its annual Apple Pie Fair then. A huge pie is baked and brought by donkey to the festival meadow. You could end August by making your own fruit pie to share with friends.

Chapter 10

September Rites and Mysteries

The "Season of mists and mellow fruitfulness" is here, as described in Keats in his poem To Autumn. For our ancestors who worked the land, September was the last good month for bringing in the grain, before the damp of October rotted what was left in the fields. Steve Roud writes in *The English Year*:

> *The importance of the harvest in an agricultural economy can hardly be overstressed... Embedded in the practical and physical arrangements necessary to 'win' the harvest... customs...grew up over the years which served to keep the workers amused, gain them some monetary advantage, or celebrate their achievements.*

These customs could have grown out of games, solutions to problems, and superstitions, but there are probably only a few grains of ancient pagan lore to be gleaned from them. Professor Ronald Hutton writes in *The Stations of the Sun* that most current ritual harvest celebrations are Christian in origin but he adds:

> *None the less, feelings persist in different forms that the season belongs to older deities as well, and this is a belief which predates... Frazer [in The Golden Bough]. Elizabethan observers of English harvest customs, after all, instinctively recalled Roman worship of the corn-goddess Ceres.*

Many modern pagans connect with the gods, goddesses, spirits of the land and seasons through folklore. Whether that's due to an atavistic memory of things otherwise lost or a modern creation is less important than the fact these things give us meaningful ways to celebrate the season. Scholars can argue whether harvest celebrations are continuations of ancient pagan festivals or are similar because they fulfil a similar social need. However, if all you want to do is honour your own gods with traditional customs, then leave the scholars to their debating, and in the words of the great philosophers Bill and Ted, "Party on, dude." There are many paganish reasons to party in September.

Dances, Games and Television

Here's the scene: six deer-men wearing reindeer antlers, a fool, a hobby horse, a bowman and Maid Marian dance around an English village to the sound of a melodeon, while people cheer them on with ale from local pubs. The Abbots Bromley Horn Dance takes place on the Monday after Wakes Sunday, closest to September 4, in the Staffordshire village of that name. This annual custom might have its origins in ancient pagan rites to ensure a good hunt. No one knows. Records show it was performed at least as far back as the Barthelmy Fair in August 1226. It's probably older. Carbon-dating showed the current antlers are from the 11th century, but might have replaced older ones. Whatever the truth, it's a fascinating event.

The Ancient Romans honoured Jupiter in a religious festival that was also a time for the Roman Games. They eventually ran from September 4 to the 19 and included chariot races, boxing and other contests. You could play games in adaptations of this celebration. The Romans were keen on boardgames such as dice, versions of checkers, and tic-tac-toe. Why not gather with friends to play these or a modern boardgame? Raise a toast to all the Roman deities then pour a libation to Jupiter, ruler of the gods.

After looking back to the past, let's look to the future. On September 8, 1966, the first episode of Star Trek was broadcast. It's celebrated annually. Early episodes had messages about equality, the futility of war, and the importance of thinking for oneself. The crew of the Enterprise offered models for problem-solving through a balance of logical thought, physical action and emotional understanding. The TV series aimed to offer a hopeful example of what the future might be like if humans follow their highest ideals. That's something we can work towards.

Autumn Walk Spell for Positivity

Sometimes we can need a bit of cheering up in the autumn. This spell often works for me. I go for a brisk walk in nature, which in the city is my local park. As I put one foot in front of the other, I repeat in my mind:

> *As I walk,*
> *I cast this spell,*
> *may all be right,*
> *may all be well.*

I visualise each step bringing my wishes closer and closer, while leaving my problems behind. Obviously, any problems also need to be dealt with in a practical way too.

Festival of the Eleusinian Mysteries

In Ancient Greece, the Eleusinian Mysteries were kept secret by the cult enacting them, but scholars believe they followed the mythic cycle of the goddesses Demeter and Persephone, and the agricultural year. A major festival of the Eleusinian Mysteries took place in mid-September, perhaps to give thanks for the harvest. It's thought the Mysteries involved an initiatory journey symbolising travel to the Underworld, offering security in the afterlife. Some Wiccan and other modern pagan witchcraft initiation ceremonies include a guided visualisation on that theme. Here's a brief retelling of Persephone's story, which you could read as part of an autumn rite.

A Tale of the Seasons

Imagine a meadow of wildflowers. In it, Demeter, goddess of the harvest, has watched over her daughter, Persephone, since she was tiny. But Persephone has grown into a young woman who wanders in search of the most beautiful flowers as her mother dozes. Suddenly the ground shakes, a fissure appears, and out of it rides Hades, lord of the Underworld, in his chariot. He sweeps Persephone off her feet and carries her away to the realm of the dead. Perhaps it's abduction, perhaps she goes willingly, the stories vary.

Distraught Demeter, in her grief, lets all plants on Earth die. It's a powerful weapon she wields. Even the gods had taken it for granted that plants would always grow, but without Demeter's blessing there's no vegetation; no food. Zeus, ruler of the gods, had underestimated her. Hades had asked his permission to take Persephone as his queen. He had allowed it without consulting the women involved. Demeter forces him to rethink and he demands Hades let Persephone go.

But that's not the end of the tale, for Persephone had eaten pomegranate seeds while in the realm of the dead. Why she ate them, again the stories vary, but Hades points out that all who eat such food are bound there. A solution is found: Persephone spends half the year as queen of the Underworld, and the other half above ground. Demeter in her turn lets plants grow in spring and summer, then die in autumn leaving the land bare in winter until her daughter returns once more the following spring.

Plant Lore

Mushrooms and Fungi

The time for mushrooms is before the frosts. Some are edible, some are poisonous, and some are magical. In folklore, fairy rings are natural circles of mushrooms in woods and meadows.

The most common is the Scotch bonnet, which gets called the fairy ring champignon. They can form because the mycelium of the fungus uses up nutrients in the soil and so expands outwards. Some British legends say the space within the ring is dangerous. If you step inside, you might anger the fae and get trapped or whisked off to fairyland for 100 years. Stonehenge is apparently encircled in a massive, ancient mushroom ring according to Sandra Lawrence in *The Magic of Mushrooms*. In France and Germany they are sometimes known as witches' circles and thought to mark places witches dance. Mushrooms are associated with witches in other ways too, particularly the red-and-white-spotted fly agaric. Its psychotropic compounds are an ingredient in old recipes for flying ointment, said to give visions and out-of-body experiences. Fly agaric is poisonous. If you see one in the woods, leave it. Don't eat any wild fungus without being sure it's safe. You won't come to harm by only taking photos.

Autumn Leaves
I love seeing the trees start to turn gold, red and brown. If you catch a falling leaf, you'll be free from colds all winter according to superstition. Another saying is that for every one you catch you'll have a lucky month the following year. Keep your caught leaves safe until new green buds appear in the spring.

Conkers
When I was a child, the dreaded return to school was offset by conker season. My friends and I would gather the huge, smooth, brown seeds of the horse-chestnut tree, prising them out of prickly cases to find the biggest, toughest nuts for games of conkers. Bouts are played by two people, each with a conker threaded on string. Players take turns to strike the other conker until one breaks. A winning conker is named after its victories. A single win is a oner, after two wins it's a twoer and so on.

The tradition can be kept alive as part of seasonal festivities, as games are a traditional part of harvest celebrations.

Berries and Fruit

Trees and bushes are usually laden with berries in September. Weather lore says exceptional abundance means a harsh winter lies ahead. Plums are among the last soft fruit to ripen, from late August to late September. In folklore they symbolise vitality and endurance. According to Rachel Patterson in *A Kitchen Witch's World of Magical Food*, plums are an aphrodisiac. Use them in spells for passion, or serve them to your beloved, perhaps in a crumble.

Michaelmas Daises

Michaelmas daisies bloom profusely at this time of year, offering food for insects and colour in the garden as the days get gloomy. Michaelmas daisies would be perfect to put on a September altar. Sandra Lawrence, in *The Witch's Garden*, writes that Michaelmas daisies are flowers of farewell – and this time of year is when we bid goodbye to summer. They are named after the Archangel Michael, whose feast day is September 29. He's honoured by followers of many spiritual paths and magical traditions. In ceremonial magic Michael can be called upon for protection. Associated with the element of fire, he's one of the guardians of the compass points of the circle, along with Raphael, Gabriel and Uriel.

World Peace Day and the Equinox

On the eve of the Equinox is the International Day of Peace. Since 1982, people have wished, prayed or otherwise worked for the absence of war and violence in the world, including temporary ceasefires for humanitarian aid. You could light a candle and visualise peaceful solutions to conflict. In the northern hemisphere the Autumn Equinox is usually on September 22 or 23. Like the Spring Equinox it's a time to celebrate balance, which I think can relate to peace. It's also another harvest celebration. Some pagans call this festival 'Mabon', but that association only started in the 1970s when American author Aidan Kelly suggested the Welsh mythological figure Mabon could be honoured then. Mabon isn't historically an autumn deity. Druids sometimes call it 'Alban Elfed', which means 'light of the water', and recognise it as a time to give thanks to the Earth for the harvest. Many pagans – including me – just call the festival Autumn Equinox.

It's fine to honour whatever deities you normally revere in your personal practice. As the light is going and colder weather lies ahead, some pagans celebrate dark goddesses such as the Cailleach, a Scottish mythological figure associated with winter. You could also honour Demeter or Persephone. We can celebrate our own personal achievements as well as balance in nature and in life. Here are some words to use in autumnal rituals:

We stand at the Equinox,
In the midst of autumn.
Dark and light are in balance,
Day and night are of equal length.
Summer lies behind us and winter before us.
It's time to take stock of our year's harvest,
To celebrate and give thanks for what we have reaped;
And to weigh up what we need for harsh times to come.
A time of joy and sadness in equal measure
Of golden memories, sweet as ripe fruit plucked from the orchard
And silver tears, bitter as the tang of fallen leaves on frost-rimed
earth.
A moment to cherish,
Like the last dance at the end of the party;
Like the last kiss before saying farewell.

Harvest Moon and Month Names

While modern witches celebrate all full moons, September's was of particular importance to our ancestors who worked the land. The full moon at this time of year can be seen almost throughout the night if the sky is clear – from shortly after sunset to sunrise. This allowed people to continue working outdoors when the sun had gone down to bring in the last of the grain harvest. Afterwards there was still light for singing and dancing in celebration.

The word 'month' relates to the moon, originally meaning the time it took for a complete cycle. The word September, however, relates to the number seven in Latin; October, November and December relate to the Latin for eight, nine and ten respectively[1]. That might be less interesting than the meanings of earlier month's names, but we're heading into the witchiest time of the year...

Chapter 11

October, Elders and the Dead

As pagans we respect the wisdom of our elders, but sometimes it's useful to have a reminder to keep in touch with our older living relatives, especially as the nights get longer and the weather colder. October 1 is International Day for Older Persons. This event to raise awareness about the problems of old age started in 1990. It reflects on a topic that's increasingly relevant as people live longer.

As well as looking up living relatives, we can think about ancestors of tradition. Two ceremonial magicians and tarot deck creators had their birthdays in October. Arthur Edward Waite, who wrote many books on magic as well as being the co-creator of Rider-Waite-Smith tarot deck, was born on October 2. Aleister Crowley was born on October 12. As well as being the founder of Thelema, he created the Thoth tarot deck along with artist Lady Frieda Harris. You could do a tarot reading for yourself, or use a card for some magic.

Tarot Card Manifesting Magic
Pick a tarot or oracle card that most represents the energy you want to manifest in your day. Study the card and visualise what you would like to happen. Put the card somewhere you can see it, and look at it to remind yourself of what you are trying to attract.

The Agricultural Cycle
The agricultural cycle always goes on, with the last of the apple harvest and the root vegetable crop being brought in. While the grain might have been harvested in September, October was

the month to start the new cycle by sowing wheat seeds for the following year, according to Steve Roud in *The English Year*.

Seed Cake

In many parts of England the time for sowing wheat was celebrated by baking seed cakes, or siblett cakes, to share with friends and family. Here's a traditional recipe from Northamptonshire:

1lb flour
1lb sugar
1lb butter
8 eggs
2oz caraway seeds
1 grated nutmeg

Beat the butter, beat in the egg whites then the yolks and finally the flour and spices. Bake the mixture in a cake tin in a hot oven for 1 and a half hours. That would make a huge cake for sharing. According to Rachel Patterson in *A Kitchen Witch's World of Magical Food*, caraway seeds are good for health, protection and fidelity magic. They can also ward against unwanted guests and the fair folk. She adds caraway seeds are perfect for use in initiation rites, so you could bake a seed cake when welcoming a new member to a coven or dedicating yourself as a witch.

Apples

Apple Day is on October 21. This modern festival, launched in 1990 by the charity Common Ground[1], celebrates the fruit and raises awareness about local varieties. It also uses the apple as a symbol of physical, cultural and genetic diversity. Magical uses include love, healing, clarity, knowledge, abundance and spirit work[2]. Apples are also excellent to use in spells to contact spirits, fairies or ancestors and are part of the traditional food and customs for Halloween.

Turnips

At one time in the UK and Ireland root vegetables, including turnips and their larger cousins, swedes, were hollowed out and turned into lanterns for Halloween rather than pumpkins. The folklore goes that they were originally put into windows to scare mischievous spirits away, rather than to indicate your home is willing to accept trick-or-treaters, as they seem to be today.

Samhain, Halloween and Mischief Night

Whether you call it Halloween, Samhain or anything else, October 31 is a major Wheel of the Year festival for modern pagans. A few traditional customs similar to Halloween take place in October in England, but their origins are unclear. Mischief Night has been celebrated at different dates in various parts of the country, sometimes on April 30 but in some places on October 31 or early November. It's a time for playing pranks, rather like trick or treat. Steve Roud, in *The English Year*, writes: "The history of Mischief Night continues to puzzle folklorists" but he adds that although "some writers have assumed an ancient pagan origin for the custom...there is no evidence that this is the case." The first documentary record dates from the 1830s, but it's likely to have happened earlier.

Halloween in its current aspect is, of course, a hugely commercialised event in Britain and more so in the United States. I find good and bad things in this. I hate the shelves of plastic tat that'll end up in landfill. It's terrible for the environment and a waste of money. But there are also brilliant things to be found in shops, from bowls and cauldrons to black candles, which are hard to get except from specialist suppliers at other times of year. So, as a witch, I look to October as a great time to stock up on supplies.

Many pagans prefer to celebrate Samhain, but the difference between Halloween and Samhain is a topic that easily get rows going. Is Halloween pagan or Christian? Is Samhain the origin of Halloween or a separate festival at the same time of year? On the face of it, Halloween is the night before the Christian festival of All Hallows Day, sometimes called All Saints' Day, on November 1. It's followed by All Souls Day on November 2, which honours the dead. But with Halloween's ghost stories, dressing up, trickery and magic, it seems pagan.

Back in the 19th and 20th centuries, many people looked at Halloween and thought they detected a festival that was ancient and pre-Christian. They looked further and saw a description of the old Irish Samhain, said to mean the end of summer, which was celebrated as a fire festival. Sir James Frazer in *The Golden Bough* had written that Samhain was a pagan Celtic feast of the dead. People put two and two together and it became accepted popular history that the origins of Halloween were in Samhain. A leaflet by the Pagan Federation in 1993 states: "Halloween developed from the Celtic Feast of Samhain."

Then some eminent historians and folklorists looked further but couldn't find evidence Samhain was to do with the dead. Some stated it was a secular new year's eve celebration at the start of winter, in which fires were lit and merriment enjoyed. Evidence that Samhain was celebrated outside Ireland was scarce, and many historians said Halloween was a different event. Roud wrote that Halloween was just a Christian festival dating from the medieval period and that Halloween was to do with the dead, but Samhain wasn't. They were different and not connected.

However, the arguments continued. A brief web search will find that the Catholic Church, under Pope Gregory III, moved All Hallows Day from May to November in the 8th century. Why was that? A popular theory is it was moved to supplant Irish Samhain, but Professor Ronald Hutton in *The Stations of the Sun* offers evidence the move was to fit in with dates celebrated in northern European churches, rather than Irish customs. Others have found connections between Samhain and Halloween. Luke Eastwood, in *Samhain: The Roots of Halloween*, searched for archaeological, historical, folkloric and literary evidence that ancestors and otherworldly beings were honoured at Samhain in Ireland, and traced ways Irish people carried their traditions to other parts of the world, to mingle with Halloween customs.

I'm convinced the arguments will continue, but I don't think it matters. Many modern pagans prefer to call this Wheel of the Year festival Samhain, while others enjoy going to Halloween parties for fun and games. Whatever you call it, you don't have to do exactly what your ancestors did unless you're a strict reconstructionist. At this time of year, when plants are dying and nights are drawing in, it's easy to believe the veil between the worlds is thin, to see ghosts in the autumn mists and hear otherworldly sighing in the winds, whatever the history books tell us. Most cultures have some sort of festival for the dead. October 31 is as good a time for modern pagans in the northern hemisphere to honour those who have died and try to contact the spirits of ancestors for wisdom or comfort.

Ancestor Altars and Dumb Suppers

An ancestor altar can be a table or shelf. On it put photographs or other mementos of family members or Craft elders who have passed. You can put flowers there and light candles and incense. Sit by your altar and talk to your loved ones as though they are present, then remain in quiet contemplation to listen for replies or messages. You can try divination, such as scrying into a cauldron of water or crystal ball, to contact those who have gone before. If you've made contact with spirits at Halloween or any other time, always thank them and say goodbye to them at the end of your session. Then make sure you are fully grounded.

Dumb suppers are special meals at which a chair and place setting are left for an ancestor's spirit to occupy while everyone else dines around the table without chatting. A candle is lit, and the ancestor invited to join the living for the meal. Everyone eats in reverential silence until the very end.

Deities of Death and Witchcraft

In my own practice I sometimes pour a libation to Hades, Greek ruler of the Underworld, at this time. As well as being a god of the dead he presides over subterranean riches including crystals. In Jungian spirituality that can be interpreted as the gems that lie in our subconscious minds. Hecate, goddess of witchcraft and the moon, can also be honoured. She stands at the crossroads with torches to light the way through darkness.

A Halloween Spell: Burying the Past

Use this spell to say goodbye to something hindering you that you no longer want in your life. Use it to get rid of unhealthy habits or difficult situations rather than individuals, as cursing people is ethically dubious and I'm not going to encourage it! Outdoors find a dead leaf. Write on it, in non-toxic ink, something you wish to be rid of. Bury the leaf, saying:

Goodbye XXX,
You were part of my life,
But now you are dead to me.
I consign you to the earth.
May you rot there.
Let there be fertile ground
For better things to grow
In the fullness of time.

Then go back inside and have a wake for whatever you have buried, perhaps with a warming drink and something nice to eat.

Chapter 12

November, Change and Transition

This month holds powerful seasonal customs even without a Wheel of the Year festival. The wheel turns and change is in the air. November 2 is All Souls' Day and the influence of this festival is wide. An All Souls' Day custom was to bake soul cakes for poor children who knocked on your door. In Catholic times, the customs aimed to help the souls of the dead, but by the 19th century this tradition was more to help the living through charity, according to Steve Roud in *The English Year*. It also turned into an adult party, with beer, mummers' plays and hobby horses – horse skulls on poles covered in a sheet. That folkloric custom can be enjoyed by anyone, and you could donate to food banks too. However, All Souls Day became overshadowed in England by Bonfire Night on November 5.

Bonfire Night and Guy Fawkes

When I was a child, Bonfire Night – or Guy Fawkes Night – was celebrated even more widely than Halloween. Originally Guy Fawkes Night commemorated foiling the Gunpowder Plot to blow up the Houses of Parliament on November 5, 1605. Guy Fawkes, a mercenary hired by Catholic conspirators to manage the explosives, was discovered and executed. Burning the image of a man with a moustache and a tall hat to represent Guy on November 5 became the custom. It's worth remembering traitors were executed by burning in England rather than witches. The death penalty for witchcraft was hanging. However, Bonfire Night has come to symbolise more than gunpowder treason. In the 19th century folklorists thought it might have ancient pagan origins. Thomas Hardy in *The Return of the Native* wrote:

Festival fires to Thor and Woden had followed on the same ground
and duly had their day. Indeed, it is pretty well known that such
blazes as this the heathmen were now enjoying are rather the lineal
descendants from jumbled Druidical rites and Saxon ceremonies
than the invention of popular feeling about Gunpowder Plot.

The Victorian folklorists were wrong, Bonfire Night itself isn't
an ancient pagan festival[1]. However, what interests me more is
the way it has been embraced as a response to what's happening
in the contemporary world. Bonfire Night only burned brightly
over the centuries because it morphed into a celebration of
riotous activity including the immolation of effigies of other
unpopular people. Effigy magic is, of course, a big part of
traditional witchcraft[2].

Bonfire Night comes on the cusp of winter and fulfills a human
need to rebel against dark times as well as have fun. Hutton
suggests this festival flourished because it's a "potent symbol".
In my own magical practice, I pay attention to potent symbols,
even if they're modern. And in recent decades the image of Guy
Fawkes himself became that of the popular rebel rather than
a traitor. Alan Moore's 1988 comic *V for Vendetta* and the 2005
film loosely based on it featured the morally ambiguous hero
who donned a Guy Fawkes mask to fight fascist oppression in a
dystopian version of contemporary Britain. The masks went on
to be worn by real-world protestors. I'm in favour of peaceful
protests rather than any causing harm, but I believe the right to
protest should be protected.

Sacrifice and Remembrance

November is Blood Month. At least the Anglo-Saxon name for
it was Blod-Monath according to the Venerable Bede. Professor
Ronald Hutton, in *The Stations of the Sun*, writes this is because
it was when cattle that couldn't be kept over winter were

slaughtered. Much of the meat was salted to preserve it, but at Martinmas, on November 11, the last of the unsalted meat was cooked for a feast to honour the necessary sacrifice in the farming year. We no longer bother about Martinmas, but Remembrance Day, also on November 11, honours those who died in war. Even during World War One the idea was the loss of life should be remembered as sacrifice and redemption rather than a celebration of victory. Armistice Day, later called Remembrance Day, commemorates the armistice signed between the Allies and Germany to end hostilities on the Western Front. It took effect at 11am – the "eleventh hour of the eleventh day of the eleventh month" – in 1918. It's an important day to remember fallen heroes the world over for Christians and pagans alike. For heathens, November 11 is Heroes Day, also remembering those who died in battle.

Poppy Symbolism and Herb Lore

Real poppies bloom in summer in England, but with its blood-red colour and short life – the blooms last only a day – it's a suitable flower to symbolise loss of young life. The corn poppy has become a symbol of Remembrance Day because the battlefields of France bloomed with them after fighting churned the ground. They also proliferated over soldiers' graves. Each year the British Royal Legion[3] sells red artificial poppies in aid of war veterans. Purple poppies remember animals exploited in wartime, especially horses[4] in the First World War. Black poppies remember the People of Colour who served in wars[5], while white poppies remember all victims of war and focus on peace[6]. You can make a knitted, paper or fabric poppy in your choice of colour to avoid buying plastic. There are free patterns and templates online and it can be an upcycling project reusing old things. Then donate money to a charity of your choice.

Poppies had been associated with death long before WW1. The flowers were thought suitable offerings for the dead in

Ancient Greece and Rome. The twin gods Hypnos and Thanatos, Greek deities of sleep and death, are often depicted crowned with poppies. Seeds can be scattered as offerings.

Rosehips

Rosehips ripen for picking after the first frosts. Collect ones that are red and soft but not shrivelled, leaving enough for birds. Rosehip tea can also be drunk before scrying to aid psychic powers. Magically, rosehips – like roses – are associated with love. For a winter love potion, add a dash of rosehip syrup to a glass of sparkling wine to share with your beloved. As a child I was more interested in the fact the fibres inside rosehips make itching powder. Wear rubber gloves if you cut hips open, and strain after cooking.

Rosemary

This herb is an evergreen with some types flowering in November in the UK. Rosemary has heaps of magical properties. Use it in spells for love, fidelity, healing, protection, sleep and memory. It's also perfect for cleansing rituals. Save some for spring cleaning next year.

Transition into Winter and Festive Preparations

Late November sees autumn's end. At the start of the month where I live there are still some leaves on the trees although many are shades of red, brown and gold. By the end of the month, following winds and rain, the oak, ash and thorn stand stark and bare. But although the nights are long and dark, we start to prepare for winter festivals. Plum puddings are traditionally made four weeks before Yuletide then allowed to mature. In England since the 18th century this was done on last Sunday before Advent – or Stir Up Sunday. If you feast at the Winter Solstice rather than on December 25 you might make a pudding earlier, but its traditions are pure folk magic. Everyone in the household is supposed to stir the mixture and make a wish. Customarily the stirring goes from east to west because that was the direction the three magi travelled after reading the stars and learning of the birth of an important child. If you don't like Bible references, you could stir clockwise for luck. Silver charms can be put in: a coin for wealth is the most common, but you could add a thimble for thrift, an anchor charm for safety, a ring for romance – or whatever's meaningful for your family. Make sure it's clean silver or it could spoil the pudding.

The commercialism of the modern festive season, and that it starts so early, gets criticism. Many don't want to even think about Yuletide until December. That's understandable, especially with concerns about excess waste. Our Roman ancestors also saw their winter festival stretching earlier. Brumalia was a festival similar to modern Christmas. It involved feasting, drinking and making merry in honour of Saturn, god of plenty, renewal and time; and Ceres, goddess of agriculture (equivalent to Greek Demeter). Bacchus the wine god was also honoured. The holiday started earlier over the years. By the Byzantine era, it began on November 24 and continued until Saturnalia, which I write about in the next chapter.

One way to escape high street commercialism is to go for a walk in nature. Even when trees are bare, there's stark beauty to be seen. You can study the bark and branches and find fallen sticks to carve into wands. Grass and fallen leaves sparkle in morning frosts and crunch underfoot. Early sunset skies can look aflame with red, orange and dusky pink. It seems hard not to believe the world and the heavens are full of magic when you see sights like these at autumn twilight. Then purple shadows lengthen with the night, and lights twinkle in welcoming windows as you head home to warmth indoors.

Autumn Guided Visualisation: Into the Darkness
The time of year when the nights are long is a good time for introspection and facing fears. This is written with that as a

theme, so you might find it scarier than the earlier visualisations in this book. I suggest reading it through before attempting it as a visualisation to decide if you want to or not. Avoid doing it if you have any mental health concerns.

Make sure you are sitting comfortably and are somewhere you won't be disturbed. Close your eyes. Take three deep breaths, in and out, and relax.

Visualise you are in an old cottage, in the country, close to a wooded hill. The cottage is sparsely furnished but comfortable, with armchairs by an open fireplace. It's an autumn night. The room is lit by the glow from the fire and a lantern, which hangs on a hook. You take the lantern and leave the cottage by the front door.

Walk down the cottage's garden path and into a country lane. A hedge rises high on either side, its leaves now gold and brown or fallen in keeping with the season. You walk, aware of your footsteps and the sounds, sights and scents of the country lane in the night-time.

After a while you come to a gate in the hedge. It's old, worn by the elements – the gales of spring, the sun of high summer, the storms of autumn and the frost of winter. Yet it's still a sturdy gate, latched and closed to all except those who know how to open it, such as yourself. Do so, notice its mechanism and the weight of the gate as you push it open. Step through. On the other side, you find yourself in a dark wood on a path winding through the trees around the base of the hill. The path is littered with fallen leaves. The night is dark, and only the glow of your lantern illuminates a few steps ahead while there is only thin moonlight and starlight overhead, glimpsed through branches.

Tread carefully. Follow the path. Push through undergrowth and twigs. The way is not easy or obvious. Obstacles are hard to see in the gloom. What sounds do you hear? Perhaps the wind, a bark, or a hoot. Keep to the path and find your way through the dark wood.

The path leads to a clearing before a cliff face at the bottom of the hill. The cliff is too steep for trees to grow on it, while the wood lies on all other sides. In the face of the cliff you see the entrance to a cave. It's to this the path leads. The cave entrance is dark. You cannot see inside. Pause for a moment, contemplating this, then step into the darkness.

What do you find in the cave? Your lantern will illuminate a small area around you – explore as you will, taking your time... Suddenly, your lantern starts to flicker. It goes out. You are in total blackness.

Then, more slowly, you realise you are able to perceive something of your surroundings. Perhaps your eyes have become attuned to the starlight through the cave's mouth, or perhaps there's a fissure above you through which the pale moon shines. Or perhaps you are using other senses to understand your environment – hearing, smell, touch, or psychic powers. Spend some time developing these senses. What do you learn in the dark cave?

Time passes. You realise you have learnt all you can this night. You leave the cave, cross the clearing, and retrace your steps on the path through the dark wood. Your developed senses help you find the way back. Now the wood does not seem so frightening. You follow the path to the old gate in the hedge, open it and pass through. Once on the lane, latch the gate behind you. Walk back along the lane, up the garden path and into the warm and comfortable cottage. Close the door and relight your lantern before hanging it again from its hook. Your journey is complete.

To return to your normal world, shake your fingers and toes, stretch your legs and arms, then open your eyes.

It's always good to eat and drink after a guided visualisation, but I would strongly recommend doing so after anything a bit scary, as well as turning your lights up brightly. Write notes in your journal. If something came up that you felt might be a mental health matter, consult a qualified professional such as your GP.

Spell: Protective Poppet for Dark Nights

You need a clean cotton fabric square ideally cut from something like an old pillowcase you've used; a few strands of your hair; rosemary or lavender; string. Place the hair and herbs in the centre of the fabric. Bunch the fabric over the stuffing to form the head with the herbs and hair inside. Tie string around the outside of the head part, to form a neck, leaving either end of the string to be the poppet's arms. The rest of the cloth, under the head and arms, represents a loose body or clothing. Enchant your poppet by saying:

By earth, air, fire, water and the power of spirit, I call my poppets to magical life. From ghosties and ghoulies and long-legged beasties, and things that go bump in the night, may my poppet protect me.

Chapter 13

December's Solstice and Yuletide Lore

So we come around to December, time to celebrate returning light in the depths of winter as well as spend time with family. But these days December is the busiest month of the year for most people, whatever their beliefs, and there's so many seasonal customs to pick from.

Deck Your Home with Evergreens

Decorating fir trees is one of the modern December customs enjoyed equally by pagans, Christians, atheists and people from many spiritual paths. We should celebrate the fact it unites us, but it also demonstrates how folk customs are constantly changing. Nowadays many put up trees at the start of December, but in the past they went up on the 24th. Christmas trees became popular in England after Queen Victoria and Prince Albert had one in 1848. In *The Stations of the Sun*, Professor Ronald Hutton writes that in England, Christmas trees were adopted as a secular and family-centric activity in the mid-19th century rather than a religious thing, meaning it became a pretty custom everyone could enjoy. Steve Roud in *The English Year* explains they were sometimes seen in England before that but weren't common.

An older way to deck the house with greenery was to hang a kissing bough from the ceiling. Roud writes: "One thing the Victorians didn't invent was kissing under the mistletoe." Kissing boughs are wooden hoops hung with greenery, especially mistletoe, and were once the centerpiece of seasonal decorations. It was said a girl would dream of her future husband if she put mistletoe under her pillow, and that the plant protected homes from lightning. In Roman times, Pliny wrote that the druids considered mistletoe sacred, so it has plenty of precedent even though kissing boughs aren't a direct continuation of ancient druidic practices.

The first weekend in December in England is National Tree Dressing Day, celebrating outdoor trees rather than firs taken indoors. It isn't an ancient pagan custom but was introduced in 1990 by environmental group Common Ground[1]. Its website says:

Trees...carry stories and put us in our place, outliving us if we let them, by many generations. In towns especially, they help to clean the air, fix carbon, reduce noise and flash flooding, provide oxygen, shade, beauty and attract wild life, yet are under constant threat from vandals, vehicles, and over-cautious councils and insurance companies. Often we take them for granted, and feel sad if we have acted too late to save them.

Tree Dressing Day draws on many seasonal, magical and spiritual customs from all over the world as well as Yuletide traditions. Some involve decorating trees, such as the Japanese practice of attaching strips of white paper, or tanzaku, bearing wishes and poems, and the Buddhist tradition of tying ribbons around the Bodhi tree in homage to Buddha. There are folkloric customs in Britain of placing tiny strips of natural fabric on branches as clooties or clouties to be disintegrated by the elements, but nowadays that's controversial. As most pagans are aware, too many well-meaning but misguided people tie manmade fabric to trees, which doesn't rot. A build-up of stuff can actually damage branches and harm wildlife if it's left there too long. This is very much against the ethos of Tree Dressing Day. You're better off putting bird food and slices of fruit outdoors for wildlife to enjoy. Common Ground says Tree Dressing Day is a chance for people to reflect on the social and cultural history of their area and the role trees have played in shaping this story. Learning where it is and isn't appropriate to dress trees, and what will help the environment rather than damage it further, can be part of that.

Holly

Before Christmas trees, people brought holly into the home. Romans decorated their villas with it for Saturnalia, which was somewhat like modern Christmas. Magically, holly has protective powers, particularly if planted around your home, and brings good luck if you hang it inside at Yule. Put it in your bedroom to help your pleasant dreams come true, and put on your altar to boost the success of your spells. However, it was traditionally considered unlucky to bring holly into the house at any time other than midwinter.

Rachel Patterson, in *A Kitchen Witch's World of Magical Herbs*, writes: "The holly berry is symbolic of the life-giving blood of the Goddess." I agree holly is a goddess tree, although many books on herbal magic list it as male. Actually, holly trees, or more accurately shrubs, can be male or female. Only female bushes have berries and they need to be close to a male bush for the flowers to be pollinated. If you have holly in your garden that never produces berries, it's a male or a lonely female. The tale of the Holly King ruling over the half the year from midsummer to midwinter, then fighting with his rival the Oak King at Yule, who defeats him to lead us back into summer, is a relatively modern myth. It comes from Robert Graves' *The White Goddess*, although he was inspired by older mythology of battling heroes.

Holly berries are poisonous, so don't eat them, and make sure they're out of reach of any pets. You can also use holly for fortune telling. Melusine Draco offers a witch's Yuletide divination using holly in her book *Traditional Witchcraft for Fields & Hedgerows*:

> If a sprig of holly is thrown on the fire and burns with a crackling noise, it is a sign that the auspices will be fine; but if it burns with a dull flame and does not crackle, it is a sign that all will not be well in the coming year.

Ivy

Holly's co-star in the carol The Holly and the Ivy is another Yuletide evergreen. The carol itself feels somewhat pagan. In *Have a Cool Yule*, Melusine Draco writes: *"...the symbolism of this anonymous early carol relates to ancient fertility mythology."* Whether or not the carol itself is ancient, Ivy is associated with both Saturn and Bacchus. Both deities were honoured by the ancient Romans with winter festivals. Worshippers of Bacchus and his Greek counterpart Dionysus carried a thyrsus – a staff wound with ivy leaves – in dances to honour their god. The staff is thought to represent male energy while the ivy symbolises female energy.

In magic, ivy represents fidelity in love. It can be used in spells to keep a partner true. Patterson writes that an ivy wreath in your home can bring in love and abundance, and keep negative energy out. Ivy flowers from September to November in the UK, and its fruits are ripe from November to January. There's usually enough of it to go around for both decorating the home and leaving outside as food and shelter for wildlife.

Death and Dark Folklore before Christmas

Crowleymass

It might seem odd to hold a party in honour of someone's death, but The Atlantis Bookshop[2] in London has a tradition of doing that to remember a famous – some would say infamous – customer. Aleister Crowley died on December 1, 1947. He's long been toasted by London's esoteric community on that anniversary.

Krampus Night

In recent years, the Krampus has become a popular character of dark folklore outside the regions he originally came from. In Germany and other central European countries on December 5, the night before the Feast of St Nicholas, the monstrous figure with horns is about. He's said to beat naughty children, put them in a sack, or even eat them, according to Al Ridenour in *The Krampus and the Old, Dark Christmas*. Krampusnacht, or Krampus Night, is nowadays an excuse for carnival-type celebrations. People dress up as the Krampus or as Frau Perchta, a Nordic folktale character and possibly an aspect of the Norse goddess Freyja. The Krampus himself is possibly a version of the son of the Norse goddess Hel, who Christians conflated with the Devil. Another suggestion is he's a dark version of the Yule Goat, a Scandinavian figure associated with the harvest and often represented in straw effigies.

St Lucya's Day and Dark Lucy Night

December 13 is St Lucya's Day. It's my name day and in Poland and nearby countries was traditionally a feast day in which a girl would parade around villages dressed in white and wearing a crown of candles, symbolising bringing light at the darkest time of the year. There's a darker side to this folk custom. Al Ridenour writes that the "dark Lucy" might be derived from the mythologies of the goddess Holda or the Slavic witch Baba Yaga. She flies through the sky with a ghostly retinue, giving fruit or presents to good children, but ripping open the bellies of naughty ones.

Kindling the Solstice Lights

People have long celebrated at around the time of the Winter Solstice, which is usually on December 21 in the northern hemisphere, although sometimes the next day. It's the shortest day of the year. Melusine Draco in *Have a Cool Yule* writes:

Winter Solstice...is the most magical and mystical time of the year and should be celebrated as such with all the pagan gusto we can summon. It is an ancient fire festival that heralds the shortest day of the year; an astronomical turning of the tide to announce the rebirth of the sun and the promise of warmth returning to the land.

96

Many of the UK and Ireland's ancient megalithic monuments align with the Winter Solstice sun, showing its importance. The rising sun shines into the central passage at Newgrange in Ireland. Maeshowe, on Orkney, lets in the light of the sunset. Stonehenge in southern England has famous solar alignments. We don't know exactly what ancient people got up to there, although archaeology at Stonehenge indicates feasting. Nevertheless, many modern pagans gather in those ancient places to celebrate the eve and dawn of the shortest day in their own ways.

One of the biggest December festivals for Ancient Romans was Saturnalia, in honour of Saturn, god of wealth, plenty, liberation and agriculture. Starting on December 17 it was a week of partying, feasting, gift-giving and drinking. People elected a 'king' to organise fun, and the Lord of Misrule in medieval courts is thought to originate in Saturnalia. Eventually it became an English household Christmas custom to elect a 'bean king' via a bean in a cake. In the 19th century vegetables were replaced by silver charms in puddings.

Even Christmas has pagan origins. While Christians celebrate the birth of Jesus on December 25, it wasn't his birthday. Hutton writes: "No modern Biblical scholars would rate the Nativity stories very highly among sources for the life of the historical Jesus." The date was already a pagan celebration by the time Christians chose the date for their festival. On that day in 274, Emperor Aurelian established the cult of Sol Invictus as an official Roman religion, and it became customary to kindle lights to celebrate the sun's rebirth. Christmas absorbed this and earlier festivals including Saturnalia. The Venerable Bede in Anglo-Saxon times stated the most important annual festival of the English had been Modranicht, or Mother Night, on December 24. It was a kind of new year event. The Scandinavian term Yule is mentioned by Snorri Sturlson in the 13th century, associated with pagan winter festivals.

Celebrating the Winter Solstice in the 21ˢᵗ Century

I love the fact that the Winter Solstice, which I mark as a spiritual event, takes place a few days before the public holiday of Christmas. It means I can celebrate with fellow pagans without that interfering with the expectations of visiting family on December 25. On the Solstice you can enact a ritual to welcome the reborn sun or honour deities, ancestors and spirits of place with words, a toast and libation before feasting and playing games. Here are other ways you can observe the Winter Solstice either on your own or with others.

Watch the Sunset and Solstice Dawn

In our modern world we're lucky to have several ways of observing this. We can travel to an ancient sacred site, stay near home to watch the sunrise or sunset on high ground with a clear view to the east or west respectively, or watch the astronomical event livestreamed from Stonehenge[3].

Personal Introspection for the Longest Night

After sunset or before dawn, turn off any artificial lights and sit quietly in the darkness. Close your eyes and meditate or contemplate what the longest night means to you. Then light a single candle or turn on a single light. Sit quietly with that for a while too and meditate further or contemplate what the renewal of light might represent to you in a personal way. Write about this in your journal or sketch your vision.

Solstice Prayer to Ancient Gods

I was inspired to write this after a Winter Solstice spent at Avebury stone circle. You can use it in your own rites, and you don't need to be at an ancient site to be there in spirit:

I say a prayer
To the ancient gods

Of the standing stones
At Solstice dawn.

I say a prayer
To the ancestors
I never knew
From the distant past

I say a prayer
To all of us
Who stand here now
As the sun returns

I say a prayer
For the world at large
In future's hope
Of brighter times.

I say a prayer
To the ancient gods
To bless us all
This Solstice dawn.

Festive Customs

Wassailing

Many of us enjoy visiting friends for drinks at Yuletide. Wassailing is one traditional way of doing this. The word comes from the Old English meaning 'good health'. Draco writes:

The mid-winter tradition of Wassailing... falls into two distinct categories: the house-visiting wassail and the orchard-visiting wassail. The house-visiting wassail is the practice of people going door-to-door, singing and offering a drink from the wassail bowl in exchange for gifts... The orchard-visiting wassail [was]...to promote a good harvest.

Orchard visiting tends to be done in January, but seasonal hospitality was earlier. Friends, family and neighbours would share a wassail bowl any time from Christmas Eve to Twelfth Night. A traditional punch was mulled ale mixed with roasted apple pulp, called lambswool. Roud writes: "Of all the [Christmas] customs that are believed to be remnants of ancient luck-bringing rituals, wassailing is the only one with any reasonable claim." Hutton points out the word 'wassail' is mentioned in the 8th century tale *Beowulf*, and the Christmas custom is recorded from the 14th century.

Yule Logs and Christmas Candles
I prefer a rolled chocolate cake at Christmas to a fruit cake covered in white icing. They're called Yule logs as descendants of the large bits of dead tree once brought into homes on Christmas Eve, or perhaps Solstice Eve, to burn throughout the long night to guard against baneful things lurking in the darkness. Sir James Frazer in *The Golden Bough* suggested it had pagan origins relating to vegetation deities and fertility. That's probably fanciful, but Hutton admits there are "traces of the sort of magical association in which Frazer was primarily interested." In Montgomeryshire the ashes were put on fields to fertilise them, while in Penistone, Derbyshire, they were put in cellars to keep witches away. The custom waned in the 19th century as fireplaces got smaller.

In 1725, historian Henry Bourne wrote about a possible connection between candles and Yule logs in Anglo-Saxon times:

Our Fore-Fathers...were wont to light up Candles of an uncommon Size, which were called Christmas-Candles, and to lay a Log of

Wood upon the Fire... It hath, in all probability, been derived from the Saxons.

However, Roud believes English Christmas candle traditions only started in the 19th century. Tradespeople gave customers large candles decorated with evergreens to put in pride of place in the home. Many Yule log customs became ascribed to Christmas candles. Lighting a Yuletide candle is still something we can do today.

Midwinter Candle Spell for Love, Joy and Hope
Here's a candle spell you can cast on Solstice Eve or Christmas Eve to help make the festive holidays perfect. You need a large, good quality container or jar candle. Choose one in red to symbolise energy and warmth, or in white to symbolise peace and reduce the chance of holiday rows.

During daylight hours, ideally at sunrise, hold the candle up to the rays of the sun and say: "May this candle be cleansed, blessed and charged by the light of the new day's sun." Bring the candle into the room you consider the heart of your home and say: "May the light of this candle bring love, joy and hope to all who dwell here, and all who visit." Light the candle at dusk or after the sun has set. Carry it into each room in the house before returning it to the main room. Put it in a safe place and let it burn during the holiday, although for safety reasons you should extinguish it when no one's around then relight it whenever you are present.

Customs for New Year's Eve
While New Year's Eve celebrations might seem non-religious, some customs are close to what our pagan ancestors got up to. Historically, New Year's Eve got a boost after the Reformation in the 16th century, when Christmas festivities came under attack as being too Catholic. In Scotland, people switched their

celebrations to December 31 and the feast got called Hogmanay. The origins of the word probably come from a French term for New Year. Hutton writes that what Lowlanders, at least, got up to was: "...much closer to the pattern of the pagan Vikings and Saxons and perhaps of the ancient British as well." One Scottish custom before New Year was saining – burning herbs including juniper as a cleansing rite – which could hark back to pagan times.

Hogmanay traditions usually include gift-giving and visiting friends and neighbours. Draco writes: "Special attention [is] given to the custom of first-footing – honouring the first guest of the New Year." It's particularly lucky if the first guest is a dark-haired man. Any who normally live in the home and match that description might get sent out into the cold and not let back in until the last stroke of midnight, ideally bringing a piece of coal – another omen of good fortune for the year to come.

Divination

I'm lucky to come from a family that did divination and fortune telling on New Year's Eve, usually after an evening of party games. We sometimes used playing cards for fortune telling or tried scrying using an old glass fishing float as a crystal ball. Scrying on New Year's Eve is a custom I still do today. The end of one year and the start of a new one is a traditional time for looking to see what the future might hold. Hutton writes that divination practices by ancient Scandinavian and Norse people lingered, demonstrated by the fact the 12th century, Bartholomew Iscanus, Bishop of Exeter, prescribed penance for those keeping the New Year with heathen rites which almost certainly included divinatory customs.

One Finnish New Year's Eve tradition still done today is fortune-telling with melted lead. The equipment to do it properly is a lump of lead, a little metal pan to melt it in, and a bowl to fill with cold water. Everyone takes it in turn to tip a little melted lead into the water. The shape it solidifies into indicates what they can expect in the year to come. You can do something similar with melted candle wax and cold water. Or, of course, you can use any fortune telling or divination system you prefer. If you use tarot, oracle cards, dark mirrors, crystals or tea leaves, try exercising your intuition rather than immediately referring to books or the internet for meanings. Trust in the magic of the universe and use your senses that aren't purely reason or logic. Pay attention to what your heart's saying as well as what your head is telling you. True witchcraft means developing your awareness there's more to life than what you can immediately see. Let your intuition be your guide.

Last Words

I started this look at the wheel of the year with January, in Chapter 2. On another New Year's Day the wheel has turned and we are there again. Except we aren't. This is a new year, a new beginning, a chance to start again – although there will be some overlaps, some repetitions. We are continuing on our path and it looks similar, but there has been a shift and we aren't walking on exactly the same ground. The wise witch who taught me said this:

> *The Wheel of the Year isn't actually a circle, it's a spiral. Each year we follow a similar path, but never quite the same. It shouldn't be identical. We shouldn't repeat the same things over and over again in an identical way. We should learn from what we did in the past and use that knowledge moving forwards.*

Look back at all you did in the year that has gone. Reread your journal, your poetry, the words of your favourite rituals. Browse again through any scrapbook, art, photographs you created. Go for a walk or look out of your window and think about what you have observed – or grown – as the seasons changed. Think about the intangible things too – memories, wishes, hopes and dreams. Congratulate yourself for all you have achieved, and give yourself a hug for any sadnesses too. Offer thanks to the deities, spirits or ancestors you worked with.

Now, look to the future, moving both onwards and upwards in that spiral. Think about what you want to continue from last year, what changes you want to make, and what ambitions you have for the year to come. Close your eyes, picture in your mind or think of words to describe how you see the way forward. Open your journal again and write that down. Light a candle and make a wish for the best that can happen in the months and seasons ahead. Remember that change is inevitable. Embrace each day and what it brings in the magic of each moment in the spiral of the years.

Endnotes

Introduction
1 johnhuntpublishing.com/blogs/moon-books/
2 philipcarr-gomm.com/essay/gerald-gardner-ross-nichols/

Chapter 1
1 www.metoffice.gov.uk/weather/learn-about/weather/seasons/
2 www.badwitch.co.uk

Chapter 2
1 londonwelsh.org/

Chapter 3
1 Starza, L, *Pagan Portals – Candle Magic*
2 blog.britishmuseum.org/whats-in-a-name-months-of-the-year/
3 Hutton, R, *The Stations of the Sun*

Chapter 4
1 Roud, S, *The Penguin Guide to the Superstitions of Britain and Ireland*
2 Theresa Dietz, S, *The Complete Language of Herbs: A Definitive and Illustrated History*
3 www.doreenvaliente.com/
4 www.wwf.org.uk/

Chapter 5
1 blog.britishmuseum.org/whats-in-a-name-months-of-the-year/

Chapter 6

1 Starza, L, *Every Day Magic – A Pagan Book of Days*
2 www.plantlife.org.uk/uk
3 Fiske, J, *Myths and Mythmakers: Old Tales and Superstitions Interpreted by Comparative Mythology*
4 blog.britishmuseum.org/whats-in-a-name-months-of-the-year/

Chapter 7

1 blog.britishmuseum.org/whats-in-a-name-months-of-the-year/
2 Wise, C, *Every Day Magic – A Pagan Book of Days*
3 www.english-heritage.org.uk/visit/places/stonehenge/things-to-do/solstice/

Chapter 8

1 blog.britishmuseum.org/whats-in-a-name-months-of-the-year/
2 Draco, M, *Every Day Magic – A Pagan Book of Days*

Chapter 9

1 blog.britishmuseum.org/whats-in-a-name-months-of-the-year/
2 https://icatcare.org/
3 https://www.cats.org.uk/

Chapter 10

1 blog.britishmuseum.org/whats-in-a-name-months-of-the-year/

Chapter 11

1 www.commonground.org.uk/apple-day/
2 Patterson, R, *A Kitchen Witch's World of Magical Food*

Chapter 12

1 Hutton, R, *The Stations of the Sun*
2 Starza, L, *Pagan Portals – Poppets and Magical Doll*s
3 www.britishlegion.org.uk/
4 https://thewarhorsememorial.org/
5 www.blackpoppyrose.org/
6 www.ppu.org.uk/

Chapter 13

1 www.commonground.org.uk/tree-dressing-day/
2 http://theatlantisbookshop.com/
3 www.english-heritage.org.uk/visit/places/stonehenge/
   things-to-do/solstice/

Readers of ebooks can buy or view any of these bestsellers by clicking on the live link in the title. Most titles are published in paperback and as an ebook. Paperbacks are available in traditional bookshops. Both print and ebook formats are available online.

Find more titles and sign up to our readers' newsletter
http://www.johnhuntpublishing.com/paganism

Follow us on Facebook
https://www.facebook.com/MoonBooks

Follow us on Instagram
https://www.instagram.com/moonbooksjhp/

Follow us on Twitter
https://twitter.com/MoonBooksJHP

Follow us on TikTok
https://www.tiktok.com/@moonbooksjhp